THE BEST POSSIBLE YOU

YOUR STEP BY STEP GUIDE TO UNLOCKING THE AWESOME POWER THAT IS YOUR INTUITION

MICHAEL DOILEY

PUBLISHED BY FASTPENCIL

Published by FastPencil
3131 Bascom Ave.
Suite 150
Campbell CA 95008 USA
info@fastpencil.com
(408) 540-7571
(408) 540-7572 (Fax)
http://www.fastpencil.com

First Edition

My dear son Max and my beautiful wife Elena; your love, faith and support is a blessing to me. This is dedicated with love and appreciation, to both of you.

Michael

❧

CONTENTS

PREFACE

Be Excited!

You are about to learn (if you haven't already) that there are no coincidences and that nothing happens by chance. You are about to see most clearly how your past has placed you at the most profound juncture of your life and why this huge leap forward that you are about to take, will be such an impressive one. Dear reader you are about to write a new destiny for yourself; be excited, your time starts right now!

The Best Possible You is about living a life of sincere internal contentment and happiness. It is an historical and modern day documentation of what must be understood to achieve TRUE success in the heart as well as in everyday life. This study focuses on ten principles, which if adhered to WILL bring to the reader an ever increasing flow of joy and success and ever decreasing feelings of fear and anxiety.

Your life is your trade and there's a good chance that so far you've been using only a rusty-old-hammer and a constantly on-the-blink torch for your life's work. You may not have realised that you have an entire warehouse full to the brim with reliable tools for your exclusive use. Your senses of sight, smell, touch and hearing merely bring you to the front gate of the majesty of your inner greatness. There is so much more!

Be excited! If you had even the slightest idea of your unlimited power, you would probably faint!

After reading and assimilating this book into your life; you will soon notice no more lost opportunities and fewer and fewer regrets. As you take on an additional perspective, even your own habitual covert self-sabotaging ways at last become clear. Using the tools within this book you will now make a future different to your past, in ways of your choosing.

Many of the characters featured in *The Best Possible You* have paid right-up-to the ultimate price in order to teach you their lessons of a lifetime. And at the same time, many individuals are in the arms of their soulmate sipping chilled champagne on board their own private yacht as you read this, happy in the knowledge that you might learn the secrets of their success.

This book requires your participation. Simply reading it is not enough to get the results you may be looking for. The more you put in, the more you will get out.

All of the stories are TRUE and I recommend you read and do the exercises in the order that they are written.

Also, please have fun with it. Generally speaking; it is our opening conversation and although the subject matter is a serious one i.e. *the reawakening of the Omni-potent human spirit after disproportionately excessive sleep,* there is still remains much to laugh about.

Fix your mind firmly on your hearts desires and disregard completely the 'size' of the task or the loftiness of your ambitions. Are looking for your soul-mate? Are you searching for your perfect career? Are you in need of confidence or self-esteem? Or is it simply financial wealth you are after? Dear reader, come with an open-mind… Of all those that have fully applied the *Ten Principles* of *The Best Possible You* to their lives I am happy to report not one single failure! Now it's your turn… But only if you BELIEVE that it is your turn.

I am not setting out to remedy every individual problem or concern with every individual person on the planet. That would be quite time consuming. Instead, my main focus is to get you (the reader) to better understand the ways of **your own** innate intuition, how it tries to help and guide you and how YOU can assist your intuition in doing its best job for you. **In effect I'm helping you in one area of your life that will assist you in ALL areas of your life**. This is because your intuition knows of all the things that truly make you happy (long-term), it knows your past and can see your potential future.

So, *am I* saying that from here on in, your life will be 'perfect?'

What I am saying is that after properly reading this book you will know precisely how to make your own life MUCH 'more' perfect and you will be more willing to allow yourself to be guided there. Your actions will no longer be governed solely by what you physically see or your painful memories of the past. You will be able to say, "*With this new information I can now see that in many ways my life was 'perfect' back then too. For it has led me to this place where I can move forward empowered, equipped with practical information making me ready and willing to do something about my standard of living on every level as well as the standard of life for those I love, right now and in the future.*"

INTRODUCTION:

What is ***The Best Possible You***?

Whilst in the Middle East, a drunken dignitary held a gun to my head and pulled back the trigger; his three body-guards stood and watched. Prior to that, I was held hostage in a 12-hour terrorist siege in Tokyo Joe's nightclub. More recently, I saved a man's life in a Chelsea Café. And some time ago I had a vivid out of body experience which, ended up with a very physical experience of milky cornflakes and marmalade flying out of my nostrils at high velocity!

Nevertheless, my life started to seriously become strange when a clairvoyant started a 'reading' for me and five minutes into the session, I took over and proceeded to tell her about her past, present and her future. I even went into graphic detail about a previous relationship she had with a man decades younger than herself. The affair happened overseas years ago and ultimately it led to her being expelled from the United States... For once it was a clairvoyant was actually speechless!

Welcome to ***The Best Possible You***, my name is Michael Doiley; you might as well call me Michael as we'll be spending some serious and some *not so* serious time together. I'm a proud husband and a proud father of one son; you'll '*meet*' Elena and Max soon.

On almost every page of this book it will be clear to see the origins of what has inspired me to write this manual. I have spent years in the Middle East, Western and Eastern Europe consciously and unconsciously registering the art of successful living and in the process becoming an expert in all things to do with 'Intuition.'

I have been blessed with the good fortune of being able to *study* hundreds of individuals from many different walks of life and even though many go unnamed throughout this book, each one has contributed in some organic way to the concept of *The Best Possible You* and the working of its *Ten Major Principles*

Half and inch beneath the skin I believe we are all *'psychic,'* how and when we come to this realisation is all that is different. For some the notion alone is scary. Before the birth of my son in 2005, I held regular meetings in different venues for those in pursuit of fine-tuning their universal sensitivity in order to get more out of life. This was in addition to my weekly one-on-one sessions in which the aim has always been to understand the inner forces that drive, direct and protect us. Some people call this force God, some call it the universe, some call it the subconscious. I believe there is a place where all these things (and more) merge together in perfect synchronisation with your unlimited success and happiness as the beneficiary; that place is your **intuition.**

By the way, I try NOT to use the word *'psychic'* too often. Not only does the word 'scare' some people but also I actually do not believe in ***'special'*** abilities. By that I mean I think that ***knowing*** other peoples thoughts is natural, ***feeling*** what others are going through is natural**.** ***Seeing*** what the future holds if a certain set of actions are followed is natural**.** ***Feeling*** that you are safe and secure in any financial, physical or emotional environment (via following an intuitive life-style), I believe is also NATURAL. I believe that we are all *psychic* and if that is the case (which it is), then it's in **no way special** to display any kind of *psychic* ability. **Most of us have simply forgotten** we have inherited abilities for **all** of the above.

For example, how often have you known someone was staring at you, even from across a busy street, across a crowded room or at a crowded venue with hundreds or thousands of people present? You just turn round and like an automatic heat-seeker missile your eyes have locked firmly onto the eyes of who it was that couldn't keep his/her eyes off you! How often have you hade a feeling in your gut that you should call a particular person, only to find out later that that person was trying to contact **you**; or that person was unwell, or simply thinking about you? How often have you made the decision not to go out, or not to go on a particular trip, only to find out later what a disaster that experience would have been for you and that your negative feelings about the event were fully justified?

All of the above occurrences are NATURAL. When they happen no one screams, no one's overly surprised. They might be *unusual* but they are still regarded as 'normal,' and that's because they are. Usually you would be complimented on following your 'gut'. ***"Oh, your ex-boyfriend was at the party last night and he was so drunk that he picked a fight with everyone! It's so good that you decided not to come, even though I asked you to."***

Just as you can train your body to be fitter, right up to olympic standard. I say the same is scientifically also true of the mind and the process of allowing your intuition to flow freely. I am happy to remind you of these natural abilities and how they can help you live a fearless, successful, happy, life.

Dear reader, as well as a motivational speaker, I am also a producer, songwriter and International professional DJ and I've spent over thirteen years deejaying in countries where English was not the first language (I've been deejaying at home and abroad since I was 14). Technically speaking, one could say that initially not being able to speak the local language was the same as losing my voice and as a consequence my other senses became heightened.

Being alone in unfamiliar lands led me to observe the subtle *and* enormous differences between the 'successes' and 'failures' around me, noticing in particular the very few who were constantly healthy, happy and prosperous.

Without the use of the spoken word I began to study body-language, attitude and other forms of non-verbal communication. Not truly knowing the intentions behind the speech or the true sentiments behind the smiles, I was forced to pay closer attention to my own instincts, intuition and my own automatic emotional responses. In addition, as I became more fascinated with the topic I read manuals, practised my own theories and continued to observe.

Still abroad, I shared some of my findings with the new people I'd met and found I was usually around 90% accurate with my assessments. I began to push the envelope further as I started to gauge family histories, financial status, health and the general disposition of my willing subjects, who were usually friends of friends looking for a novel time to spend an evening. But when I was able to give a plan of action for life-turnarounds, as well as point at a particular feature of someone's history or recurrent behavioural pattern and say, *"Change that and you change your life."* Then all of a sudden those who had sent their friends to me for a bit of fun, were now *themselves* being sent back to me for a life-altering experience!

I had found that for many of us, there exists dominant belief systems in specific areas of life that act like a drug to numb that area into a sleep-like state, consequently restricting us from experiencing the fullness of relationships, work, family, self-esteem, financial freedom or the whole package of ***'life'*** itself.

Often, though not always, it starts with demeaning words or negative actions experienced from parents or peers or persons whose opinions you hold in high esteem. Ultimately though, it doesn't so much matter how the process was initialised, **what matters most is that you believed it.**

Suffice to say, that if you have a way of thinking about yourself that does not empower you, but instead slows you down in mind or body and makes you feel either powerless, unworthy, unloved or *un*-dynamic, then this is what I am referring to.

Alas, now as we find ourselves in the midst of a new financial depression, more and more people are looking for a way to lift their heads out of this bottomless pit of gloom. To see a sparkling future image of themselves that reminds them of the truth they knew about themselves before they made the money that they then lost. But it's not just about money and neither is this book.

Now it's all about you and how you view yourself. For in what I have witnessed and experienced; I have learned that you cannot expect the world, or indeed other individuals to change simply because you want them to, and getting them to change is often missing the point. For I know without a shadow of a doubt that where you are right now and who you have around you at this very moment forms the perfect launch-point for your ***shining destiny*** to meet you as immediately and as fully as is possible.

Within the pages of *The Best Possible You,* you will get to clearly see the effects of (often) invisible self-negating habits and belief systems that may have given you only half a life (in most cases even less than that). And at the same time I present to you empowering true-life stories of popular public figures, heroes and villains who throughout history have unwittingly shown us the ***Ten Major Principles*** of ***The Best Possible You*** in action and the awesome life-affirming benefits the principles have to offer.

This book has seen professional critiques; it has had three incarnations and diligently and patiently the book itself has taken twenty-years to obtain the synchronicity of content, purpose and relevance needed for its most poignant timing. In many ways, the book waited for me to mature so that I could finish it. But throughout the years it never gave up on me and never let me off the hook.

Upon noticing how the general pubic lavish attention on soap stars, sports people and celebrities, I've decided to involve well-known personalities in my study, and I've focused in depth at the often unseen attributes that have taken these individuals to fame, fortune and power. These insightful experience-based anecdotes and quotes I have personally found fascinating and I believe deserve to be shared. Learning how others deal with their 'demons' and other personal challenging issues helps put a human face on the often 'scientific' exercises. It also assists me in conveying my belief that *'spiritual'* growth need not be exclusively for the *'spiritually'* minded, and triumph through adversity is not a trait solely assigned to the Generals of World War II. To lose weight is a triumph, to raise a child is a triumph and so too is climbing your own personal mountain.

My passion and sincerity is carved into each word on each page. It has been inspired by every one of the hundreds of people that I have personally crossed paths with or was **intuitively** led to study.

This is a gift to all you if you feel you have yet to reach your potential. It's for you if you desire a future more loving, more successful and more satisfying than your past. It's also for you if you believe the best possible you has yet to be seen.

1

CHAPTER 1: SIGHT CAN BE DISTRACTING

(*Principle 1* : Open-mindedness)

Sight can be Distracting... Be Open-Minded.

"The first sign of madness is doing the same thing over and over again and expecting a different result". Albert Einstein (14th March 1879-18th April 1955)

Therefore, if you want changes in your life, you must be prepared to try new and different things. To try different things you must first be open-minded. Ultimately, you must be open-minded about allowing success and all manner of good things to flow uninterrupted into your life. But these wonderful things may not all look wonderful when you first see them, they may not sound wonderful or feel wonderful. This is why being open-minded is so crucial; your hearts desires could slip right through you fingers because you are not prepared for they way they look, sound or feel.

It is with good reason thatt Open-mindedness is the first major principal in the **10 principles of the *Best Possible You*** (BPY). And quite frankly, without it, you need not purchase this book, it is THAT fundamental.

"How far back does it go?
To the very beginning of time,

For when you emerged from your mother's womb,
The first thing you did was cry,
You were given the gift of life,
And did you appreciate it?
You may laugh now,
But back then you hated it!
And where would you be if you couldn't eat?
I hear you laugh again.
But every one of those thirty-odd teeth caused you endless nights of pain.
Do you yet understand,
The beauty hidden in the pain,
Of growing.
Fairy tales make us believe love looks a certain way,
And if I gave you an unpolished diamond,
You just might throw it away?
Would you walk past your favourite store,
If they changed their carrier bags?
Would you notice your Prince Charming,
If he was dressed like a pauper in rags.
Do not be deceived by presentations,
Don't be distracted by the pretty pink bow.
For to truly understand the gifts life brings,
There's something we all need to know.
Love can sometimes look ugly,
Love can even feel like pain.
Love often plays tricks with our emotions
Just to see if we'll turn away

Even without the financial depression that we find ourselves in, it would still be time to be open-minded about the TOTAL sum of ALL your parts. Awake dear reader Awake! You have talents and skills that you may not have even begun to learn yet, but your aptitude and compatibility for them are perfect.

You are not your business card and that, now more than ever, really is the point. You are infinitely more than a few words put together on a piece of paper smaller than a pork-chop. It's like putting a rainbow next to a brick. And by the same token, **you are also more than just a body.** Your hopes and fears, your talents and skills, your beliefs and your eternal spirit are represented in the most minimalistic of ways by your body and more often than not, not represented at all. As it is displayed most vividly in the case of perennial genius...

Stephen Hawking, (born 8th January 1942) CH, CBE, FRS, FRSA whose impassioned research into black holes, radiation, cosmology, quantum gravity and other complicated things have made him a giant amongst men. Stephen has suffered from ALS (Amyotrophic lateral sclerosis) since the late 1960's and his severe state of paralysis has meant that he has been unable to move or indeed feed himself since 1974. To look at him is one thing, but Stephen Hawking is more than a body, his research will tell you that and so too will his adoring children, Robert, Lucy and Timothy.

"My goal is simple. It is a complete understanding of the universe, why it is as it is and why it exists at all."

As quoted in *Stephen Hawking's Universe,* by John Boslough.

Stephen is one of the most inspiring people of all time, not just because of his landmark discoveries, but also because he represents the truth about us all. In 1974, doctors gave Stephen barely 10 years to live, but he has decided to live as long as he wants to. Hawking is motivated by the love of his family and his lifelong obsession with the workings of the universe, his body is not a great deal more than a reference point to help us give a name to where a particular idea came from. And that goes for the rest of us too. Even in the 21st Century, we are still so wrapped up in the exterior of all that we look at, distracted by it to our detriment.

It's all about perception, sight can be distracting, what we see, what we think we see, and what those images mean to us. The world cannot all of a sudden be poor and you cannot all of a sudden be worthless! Do not be depressed be open-minded. You were precious even before birth, as you are precious even after our so-called *death.* Whilst living, you have countless opportunities to show the multitude of different ways why you are not only precious but also an **essential** piece of the jigsaw we call life. Being *sacked,* being *dumped,* being evicted, are all exterior views that in reality are seen only by the body's eyes. **Intuition** never loses sight of your worth nor the worth of others. Resurrected careers of movie giants like Jeff Bridges, John Travolta, Alec Baldwin, Mickey Rourke and Robert Downey Jnr remind us only that with Faith, a period of time in 'limbo' need not last forever, it can even be useful when staging a comeback. After all, you can't have a fanfare and bunting 'comeback' if you're always 'there.' What looks like a 'finished' actor to one director is the passport to Oscar glory for an open-minded director, aka *True Grit, Iron Man, The Wrestler, Pulp Fiction* and *30 Rock*. **You** may or may not win an Oscar, but my friend you are FAR from finished.

You are alive! And 'if you're alive it means you have something to do. Something ONLY you can do, ***even*** if it looks like something similar to what someone else has done or is doing.

Have Faith, trust what your intuition says and close your eyes to properly view the situation that is causing you anxiety or slowing you down… Sight can be distracting. Use vision instead. Your **vision** for your future may have NOTHING in common with your present. But may simply be how things can be if you apply yourself fully to the situation by navigating your route via your **Intuition**.

The world's financial situation is the distracting spin-off from the main program that has eclipsed the main program in terms of its audience numbers and concerned viewers. It's the Ben Johnson steroid saga of the 1988 Seoul Olympics, but not the Olympics. It's the David Beckham sending off in the 1998 World cup in France, but not the world cup. It's the colour of the President's face in the 44th US presidential election of 2009, but not the changing face of America. And it's the crucifixion of Jesus Christ at 3pm April 3rd 33A.D, but not His resurrection. It goes without saying, that anyone can be killed; and throughout history thousands have been crucified. Nevertheless, our upside down sense of what is important has meant that we have upheld the disturbing image of a man's brutal murder more than looking at the possibility that a human-being can defeat mankind's most poignant of 'full-stops' and casually walk past his most *final* of all resting places… the grave.

If you have even a passing interest in the Bible you'll understand that the wearing and the purchasing of crucifixes over the centuries show exactly what part of the story the general public has an obsession with. As for me, the thought that a man can perhaps nonchalantly drop in on old friends three days after being killed, complete with nail holes in his hands and feet; well... I tend to find that sort of thing particularly intriguing and inspiring.

Back to more recent times and we find that money like the crucifix has elbowed its way centre-stage in an audacious bid for instant stardom. But alas, money has no talent whatsoever and the judges will eventually realise that. All it ever really does is follow. It sinks in a recession and jumps up in a recovery. It moves like Jagger when stimulated and does nothing when it is ignored. It doesn't love you or hate you and will leave you as easily as meet you. It stays by your side only when it has others like itself for company and it feels just as at home in a tin cup as it does in a vaulted bank.

Still, the collapse of *money* has now already taken place and typical of all bad losers it wants to drag everything that it can down with it. And just like the toppling of Saddam Hussein's' statue in Firdos Square, Baghdad, in April 2003; *money's* legs are broken and great change is afoot.

However, rich and poor need not be afraid... A new leader is about to be quickly installed and she will place members of her own family in office around her. Her name is *Self.* (In China, where the economy is presently in steady growth, family names precede first names this is also the case with *Self).* She will bring into the fold her strong siblings; *Self-Worth, Self-Reliance and Self-Preserve.* She also has at her side her staunch deputy, *Self-Belief.* It has been stated quite firmly that *Self-Indulgence* still has a role to play in this new government, but his outlandish spending will be under close scrutiny by international inspectors amid fears of previous budgetary **Maths Destruction.**

THE END of THE WORLD?

The astronomers of the ancient (highly) advanced civilisation of Central America, known as the Mayans (AD 300-900) created a complex detailed calendar based on cycles of 144,000 days. These cycles were called Baktoons. A great deal of money and anxiety has been made by the crude misrepresentation of the Mayan calendar which clearly states we will enter into a new cycle of creation at midnight on 21st December 2012 (the 13th Baktoon). Nowhere on this calendar does it say the world will end! Every Mayan professor will attest to this and every native Guatemalan will laugh in your face if you ask about the world ending in 2012. So, a new way of thinking? I think yes. New perspectives? I think yes. Perhaps even new world leaders and a re-shuffle of the world's leading nations with the likely re-introduction of gold-linked currencies to be kick-started by a Middle-Eastern or West African country, where gold stocks are plentiful. To all these things, most probably 'yes' and 'yes' to other things too, but the end of the world... No, I don't think so.

How often have we all wished that we had the knowledge we have now, but when we were much, much younger? The world is in the process of being reborn, so now we *all* have wise heads on young shoulders. Yes, there will be some tears (actually... a lot of tears), **but** certainly not as much as the first time you came into the world. How often have we wished for a more level playing field where talent, goodness, perseverance, endeavour, creativity and imagination would have the equivalent value or more value than money? Now it does! There are millions of people whose talents have been lying dormant under the cover of a blanket of Dollar bills, Pounds and Euros. The wake-up call rings loud now and the Ministry of *Self-Expression* has already issued grants and permits to all, do not squander yours.

Dear reader, you may not even wish to consider it now, but how lucky are you? This is a brave new planet that is giving you a second chance. You are presented with countless opportunities to start over and try out your ideas on a public that are in dire need of fresh new ideas.

Western civilisation has found itself in a financial mess; can *you* make a fresh deposit of bankable innovation? Global warming has given our planet a curable cancer; the antidote could be in the Rain forests, your back garden or in your very own conscious or subconscious mind? Yesterday, when I glanced over the markets I noticed that nearly **all** the major financial institutions were taking a fierce hammering; banks, building societies, the *Dow Jones,* the *FTSE, the Euro* etc, etc. The car industry too was taking some dangerously deep dents, the impact of which could not be remedied by air-bags no matter how large. *Ford* and *General Motors* in particular suffered serious scratches to an age-old infrastructure... But, however, pharmaceuticals were up and so too was *cocoa*... **aspirins and chocolate**. Surely, that cannot be a surprise? Once failing coffee chain *Starbucks* are continuing to grind out a formidable rise. *Apple* products remain at legendary must-have status, high-end retailer The *John Lewis* group march onwards and upwards in profits with their staff owned establishment and as we speak, business for the *super* high-end *Rolls Royce* is up by 30% in the UK and 46% worldwide! Remember, these vehicles (Ghost and Phantom models) are selling for 174,950.00 to 349, 950.00 British Pounds ... each!

Do not let anyone tell you that there is no longer money 'out there'. I recently Deejayed at a gig where the company hosting the evening splashed out on twenty-two new chauffeur driven *Rolls Royces* to usher their executives to the the venue! Park Lane in London is used to seeing over the top glamour, but I must say that was a sight to behold.

Has your intuition started pulling at you yet? Has your subcon scious started stirring? Soon, friend soon. So, what do you have, what can you do, what can you say, what can you paint, what can you write, what can you design, what can you stitch, what can you dance or choreograph, what can you sing, play, make or teach that can give the world distraction, relief or remedy from the grey cloud of gloom that hangs overhead? Still, I'm not speaking about the ENTIRE world being under a grey cloud. As we speak, China, Brazil, India, Indonesia, Iran, Russia, Venezuela and others have moved into the VIP lounge and are taking their seats. Whilst simultaneously other countries are being shown the door, but not without a great deal of fuss about settling their bills before they leave.

With an open mind, this may ALL be to your benefit. For you have something the world needs, if only you believed in yourself enough to give it a try. For whatever it is, it just might make you very rich indeed ... and this time you will be rich in **soul** as well as in the bank. For you will also intentionally or unintentionally remind others of *Self* and in so doing you'll help *Self-Esteem* get back into office, from where it has been exiled for so long. Your expressive soul has been asleep for such a long time that you may have even temporarily forgotten what your real talents are ... the hibernation is almost over, throw away your business card (metaphorically speaking of course), for you are so much, much more than that.

2

Chapter 2: Intuition: (We have Forgotten More than we Know)

The Best Possible You is comprised of **Ten Major Principles**; the second of which *(Principle: 2)* is **INTUITION:** It is your Crash helmet, safety-net, air-bag, foam padding, stop sign, go sign, adviser, contraception and your all-round best friend.

Successful seasoned stock market traders use intuition when the market goes up or down and they make bucket loads of money either way. The dewy eyed romantic uses it the first time he spots the *'love of his life'* twenty paces across a crowded dimly lit room. And clever motorists use it when trying to find a parking space in central London on a Saturday afternoon during *'Sale'* time. These sometimes playful uses merely form the tip of the iceberg of what your intuition, otherwise known as *gut- feeling,* instinct or *6th Sense* is actually capable of.

Albert Einstein wrote: "***The intuitive mind is a sacred gift and the rational mind is a faithful servant. We have created a society that honours the servant but has forgotten the gift.***" *Now where have you seen that before?*

Intuition is one of the **Ten Major Principles** of *The Best Possible You* and is one of the fundamental cornerstones of what this book is all about. I will explain why you need it now more than ever and more importantly how to harness this awesome tool of unimaginable proportions to climb to the highest of heights in your chosen vocation, and how to make masses of money or attain your hearts desires in any other area.

On the subject of the 6th Sense, *yes,* I can see dead people and I see them everyday. Most of them do not even know they are dead... Don't get me wrong, they are not *physically* dead; they're not *ghosts* as in the Hollywood movie starring Patrick Swayze or the really scary one starring Bruce Willis. These people eat, talk, breathe, work and have no death certificate. But their existence should not be classified as living, as they are as close to the living *dead* as is possible without actually being deceased. For all intents and purposes, they are asleep, **hibernating**, until... God only knows when.

Utilising your intuition is one of the most important steps toward ending this hibernation. It is the initial spark which may inspire your entire being toward certain success. It is a long forgotten art and potential lifesaver. It is a resurrection for the dormant soul itself.

The main reason why it's so important is that it comes from an altogether different place to where all your other decisions are made i.e. your logic based brain or your body. Can you make decisions from the body? We make decisions based on what we think our bodies need. The body, for example sends impulse messages to the brain to tell it that it is hungry, it doesn't happen the other way around. Or when you put your hand near a fire, your receptors and nervous system tells the brain you feel heat and programmed responses make sure you move your hand quickly away. Intuition however can bypass all of your usual bodily functions. It can see past what we commonly term as sight, it can enhance or block what we believe is sound, and the information it can convey to us is profoundly more meaningful than what our noses and fingertips by comparison 'primitively' show.

Please do not take what I have written lightly for intuition is a tool that can win wars against all odds; David's slingshot strike against the forehead of Goliath or the Allied capture of Normandy during *World War II* were motivated **more** by intuition than meticulous calculation. In 1928 when Scottish bacteriologist Alexander Fleming (1881-1955) noticed that a mould had formed on one of the cultures he was working on in his laboratory, he was at first tempted to simply discard it as something worthy only of the waste-paper bin. But **intuition** slowed his hand and guided him instead to further study this strange mould that seemed to be dissolving the bacteria surrounding it in the Petri dish. Soon it became apparent that Fleming had unearthed perhaps the most powerful medicinal tool of the 20th Century, for his intuition had led him to the discovery of Penicillin. Millions owe their lives or well-being to his miraculous find.

The world's second richest self-made billionaire Bill Gates actually dropped out of the world's most prestigious university Harvard, because his **intuition** forcefully told him that his work on computer software could wait no longer. At the time his parents may not have been too impressed with his decision although I would imagine that by now they would have come to appreciate their son's independent way of thinking.

Intuition told my wife Elena, that the skin condition that our son was suffering from was not simple *"... childhood eczema"* as most of the doctors dutifully told us. They also said that he would grow out of it by the time he was six or at the latest nine years-old. It was then that my wife made her own pledge to find a speedier cure for our boy who was only a year-old at the time and was in such extreme discomfort that if left alone for **even a very brief moment** would scratch his face and head until blood ran down it. Advice from experts as far apart as China, Australia, France and the UK got us on the right track as we finally realised our son had a host of different allergies to various foodstuffs. These included: wheat, soya, eggs, milk, nuts, fish, food additives and colorants as well as allergies to grass pollen, tree pollen, dust and carpet fluff; 12 in all. Nevertheless, with a completely customised organic diet (managed by his mother) as well as lotions, face and body creams (concocted researched and mixed by his mother) I'm happy to say that just one year later, at the ripe old age of two, my son Maximillian had no signs of eczema on any part of his body! He gained weight because he was allowed to sleep at night without the constant itching of his entire being. His hair now grows as glossy and as full as any normal child because he is no longer endlessly scratching it, damaging the scalp and follicles in the process. And in every area that needs concentration he has begun to excel because he is no longer constantly distracted by the feeling close to that of a hundred bees crawling up and down his skin, stinging at random. All because of his determined mother's **intuition** and her complete willingness to listen to her inner *voice* even when the dark clouds (doctors/experts) had blocked her view so 'completely'. I am proud of my wife for many things, but giving quality of life to our beloved son, especially in his formative years, showed me the true depth of *my own* blessings and the accuracy of **my own intuition** for making her my wife in the first place.

Intuition can bring down giants, win World Wars, heal the population of an entire planet, help a baby to grow happy and healthy and inspire admiration from an already doting husband. This is intuition; this is your gift, your road to riches, your escape from danger and your path to enduring love. Let me help you to develop yours and then follow it as you watch the universe bend and fold in it's accommodation of your wishes.

Alternatively, you can close this book right now and lead an ordinary life. The choice is yours.

So you've decided against an ordinary life… Wise choice; let us then begin.

.

Michael Doiley's Qualifications

Because you have an intelligent enquiring mind, you will by now want to know what manner of formal qualifications has the author acquired which gives him the right to spread his way of looking at the world? The answer to that question would be no *formal* qualifications. I have *no* qualification in psychology or philosophy and my keen interest in history is purely of my own volition as it has helped me to make some sense out of the phenomenon that I have personally witnessed during the past fifteen to twenty years of putting this book together. Nevertheless, even though many might view having no board certified recognised qualifications associated with my studies as a disadvantage, I personally choose to see it as a definite **advantage**. This is because what I disclose to you is based on what I have personally experienced and researched and not merely ***Other People's Logic***. It's what I have witnessed first hand and what has been brought to me in my capacity as a coach, motivator and friend. I am not reading from centuries old passed down information that does not acknowledge electricity, the internet, ease of travel and various new forms of learning media. No nine to four schooling system has dictated what you are reading. And while I believe a good college education is great, I do not believe it is *essential* for your impending great*ness*. Amongst many high achievers, both Bill Gates and Roman Abramovich, dropped out of college and did rather well in their chosen vocations regardless. And the great Winston Churchill once said,

"My education was interrupted only by my schooling."

You have your own path, it may include years of schooling and it may not, but not having a college degree is not an excuse that will be acknowledged as a reason for lack of achievement in your present or future. Forbes magazine announced in 2007 that Croydon born Supermodel Kate Moss is now the 99th richest woman in Britain with a fortune of over 45million pounds sterling. Not bad for self-made woman in her early thirties who not only never went near a university (apart from driving by one in a taxi or limousine) but she also never did particularly well in high school, achieving mainly C's D's and F's in her GCSE's. People have said, *"She has a gift," She's extraordinarily beautiful," "There's no one else in the world like her."* Every one of those sentiments applies also to you too, even if you're not from the sunny district of Croydon. You have a gift (many gifts), you are extraordinarily beautiful (in ways you may yet discover) and without doubt there is no one else in the world quite like you (no one else has your thoughts, your unique personal history, your skills, your perspectives, or your individual character).

I have drifted ever so slightly but no, I do not have a Bachelors Degree in *Speaking Your Mind* and I don't have a diploma in *Spreading Good News,* I just do it. And I do repeat that while I do believe a good extensive school education is great, (it certainly helped one Barrack H. Obama) I do not believe it is *absolutely essential* for learning, passing on information or indeed success... **What is essential is that you do all that you can to learn whatever you need to make your own life work in terms that YOU are satisfied with.** These things may well require schooling, mentoring, reading or some kind of out of school coursework but whatever the case may be, it should be in line with your goal for success. Author *Napoleon Hill* wrote in his classic *"Think and Grow Rich."*

"Any person who is educated is one who has learned to get whatever he wants in life without violating the rights of others. Education consists, not so much of knowledge, but of knowledge effectively and persistently applied. Men are paid not merely for what they know, but particularly for what they do with what they know."

Aside from meditation, there are countless ways in which you can stimulate your **intuition** to have it work for you in a more efficient manner. A well-known ground level intuition muscle-builder is 'seeing' your parking space in your mind's eye before reaching it. In other words, when you are driving around, especially in town, instead of panicking, picture your parking space, choose it in your mind (or have your mind choose it for you). If you get to the vicinity of the space and there are no vacant spaces, with time you can challenge yourself by putting on your hazard lights and staying put for a minute until your space appears. Perfection comes with time… and a little faith

If you really want to jump-start your intuition into gear, then the *Stretch and Shrink* meditation below; will be very helpful:

STRETCH ANDSHRINK

Before you begin this exercise, be sure that you are quite familiar with the room that you are meditating in, get comfortable, close your eyes and begin.

Say a prayer or do whatever you personally like to do to get yourself into a calm meditative state of being and then with your eyes closed imagine that you are growing. See yourself steadily getting taller and broader and with it notice how your perspectives of the room begin to change. Now you can see clearly all that's on top of the ward-robes followed by a new view of all the dust above your light fittings. As you imagine your head bending to accommodate the ceiling, you now realise that your growing body is no longer solid and like an upward periscope you are easily able to grow through the ceiling to see all

that's going on in the room upstairs. Eventually, you find yourself standing with your entire home below you by your ankles and the view you have of your city/town is quite spectacular, understandably you think this is cool. A bird might fly past your ear and you'll also notice how slowly everything on the ground seems to move when you are so far up.

Once you are satisfied that you've seen enough, it is then time to shrink back down, but do it slowly and progressively; through the rooftop, view the attic, through the rooms or above flats, back to the room you are sitting in with the above wardrobe view, back to you normal size. But don't open your eyes just yet, for it is time for you to shrink further.

As you continue the shrinking process, notice that you have to stand away from what you're sitting on otherwise you'd tip over. Shortly you are small enough to see beneath the chair and any table that might be in the room. Then you become small enough to see underneath the bed and soon you are so small that you can actually see the individual carpet fibres and small enough to fall down a gap between two planks of wood that would form your floor boards. The landscape is incredible, even if a little intimidating. It feels as if you are on a different planet, where your chair is taller than the Empire State Building and a fly would sound like a helicopter and look like a Good-year sponsored hot air balloon, amazing stuff.

Once satisfied, breathe out, it is time to grow again so you walk away from under your chair so as not to bump your head on it as you regain your normal size.

Slowly, as if you are going up in a glass elevator, your view changes and changes until you are the perfect size to sit back down in your original seat. Now refreshed, slowly open your eyes.

*

The "*stretch and shrink*" exercise, as well as all the other forms of visualisations and meditations that I will show you, are symbolic directives to your subconscious, telling it that you are open to view your life from another perspective. Just as smoking the peace pipe with Ancient American Indians indicated the willingness for peace and open communication, so does this kind of exercise show your subconscious, (**the home of your intuition**), that you no longer wish to fight it, and that you too are open for communication.

*

Acknowledgement of your intuition is a lifestyle, for some individuals '*oneness*' with the subconscious may take years to master. For others it need only take a short while, for your subconscious and all it entails are closer to you than your own heartbeat. Acknowledge your power each day by sending blessings and positive thoughts of appreciation and gratitude to God or the Universe. This can be done just before sleeping or upon waking or in fact any time of day, as often as you like. It can be part of a prayer, a positive affirmation, a short meditation or whatever is comfortable for you.

For just as the suns rays warm the planets of our solar system, so too do your loving thoughts radiate forever outwards, placing you at the centre of your own universe with goodness, inspiration, love, miracles, and joy all in gentle orbit around you; waiting to drift closer to you as they gravitationally pull upon your day. Then reflecting back upon you all throughout the day are your magnified intentions, desires and projections. Intuition behaves like fiery comets or small shooting stars flashing gloriously across your line of vision as you go about your day, lighting up your mood when you need the inspiration most.

Unfortunately, all of this also applies to negativity as well… This means your negative desires and negative intentions, to cause harm, hurt or to destroy are also placed in orbit around you, by you, waiting for the opportune moment to revisit their maker. Some call it karma. In their series of groundbreaking publications, Esther and Jerry Hicks have labelled it the *"Law of Attraction."* And in his way–ahead-of-its-time masterpiece, *"Think and Grow Rich"* Napoleon Hill called it *"Kickback."* It all works on the premise that everything in our universe can be ultimately broken down into naked–to-the-human eye electrical vibrating particles that move at different speeds depending upon their density. These particles form the molecular building blocks of everything known and unknown to man and are the very fibre of thought itself. To bring the things you want into your life, you must train your mind to reach a certain vibration around the particular thought/ desire in order to attract it, or its' equivalent. This means that whether you like it or not, thoughts that have at their base jealousy, anger, fear, attack, revenge, aggression, hatred and their like, can eventually reap havoc in your own life when these thoughts are allowed to gather momentum and go unchecked.

Prolonged negative thought patterns are harmful to the thinker even if the vicious fantasies are never carried out in reality. Months or years of reminiscing on wrong that has been committed to you, pontificating or verbalising revenge scenarios and even harbouring guilt feelings over what you may have done in the recent or distant past is extremely detrimental to your **own** health. Because you are in essence creating the vibration necessary to bring all that you are concentrating on, into your own life**. It's not what you see or do, but it'swhat you constantly think about that will determine your destiny**. And therefore if you are constantly thinking about hurting someone, you will at some point find yourself hurt in the same way (or worse) because the universe believes that all that you request, you request for yourself, and obligingly it gives you what you ask for. And you ask for something by thinking about it in a passionate-vibration-stirring way (that we will go into more detail about later). But, I hasten to say, **if dealt with in time, all negative 'kick-back' consequences can be halted,** thank heavens.

...For example, just consider for a moment how many times you have tripped over, or stubbed your toe, bruised yourself, cut yourself or accidentally hurt yourself whenever you are in a rage or particularly angry with someone.

Your intuition is your own personal security system. It looks after your well-being and the well-being of those close to you.

- Just like your body, your intuitive muscles need regular workouts. For fun guess bus, train, taxi arrival times. Guess the background and occupation of people you meet (as a game). Guess who will be the next person to walk in through the door or what he or she will look like.
- Listen to your 'gut'. Intuition becomes stronger only when you acknowledge it. Ignoring it makes it weaker.

- ❊ If you are about to do something or say something and you get an unexpected interruption before you are able to do so- Pause, Stop and think. Ask yourself if what you are about to do or say is entirely necessary, or could it possibly wait for further thought? Should you even consider not saying or doing what it is that you almost did/said. Often intuition gets additional assistance from the universe-at-large, be sure to notice it.
- ❊ Your Intuition looks out for the things that you give your regularly give attention to or/and feel passionately about.
- ❊ Meditate. Little but often. Doing five to ten minutes a day of meditation five times per week is extremely beneficial as it calms down your thoughts making your mind like a steady gently flowing river, where any ripple-causing 'debris' or inconsistency is easily noticed.
- ❊ Visualise: Use your mind to picture **future** outcomes of **present** decisions. You will be giving your intuition a moment to help you. When I was 20-years old, an ex-girlfriend showed up on my doorstep wanting to have passionate sex with me that night even though I had not seen her or heard from her in over two years! She came from a very religious family and when we were originally together we had a great relationship that lasted over a year but we never had sex. As beautiful and as enticing as she was that night, something inside me made me say no; and for that crazy evening I stuck to my ***guns*** (and certainly fired no shots!). We chatted for a while, I peeled her off my neck, and then she left. Months later I learned she was pregnant at the time she visited me. As naïve as I was, I would have most certainly believed I was the father and as this was before I started travelling, my life would have been 180 degrees different to what it is now*. This experience was the first jolt to my system that made me aware **of what a guiding formidable force the intuition can be.**

Intuition is so invaluable because it goes beyond what is on the surface, in fact its best utilised with eyes shut and with time the gifts that it brings contain the answers to all of your questions. When allowed, it sometimes brings with it, vivid glimpses into your not-to-distant future. For it is the outstretched fingertips of your all-seeing all-knowing subconscious, reaching back from eternity to contact you with all the answers you seek in the **now** of time. It comes from a place not of the body, somehow outside your physicality; yet its'connections necessitate that it only wants what is best for your-***self.*** Being guided through seeming darkness (problems) and into light is not a problem, for the navigational system used by intuition is second to none and requires only that your mind remain open even when you have closed your eyes in fear... of a catastrophe...

3

Chapter 3: Chinese Catastrophe's

In a relatively short space of time, sublime songstress **Adele,** has been immortalised and shunted into legendary status by her phenomenal 6-Grammy haul at the prestigious **Grammy Awards** of **2012**.

To date (Feb 2012) her amazing album ***21*** has been in the world-wide charts for 52 weeks and at number one for 31 weeks. Her heartfelt lyrics and soulful voice has undoubtedly touched the heart and soul of the entire planet and as a result she won everything that she was nominated for and sold 17 million copies of her album in the process!

This means the 23-year-old has more Grammy's than the **Beatles** and is an inspiring international superstar because of her experience of the **Chinese Catastrophe**'.

I'll explain: In Chinese (writing) calligraphy, the word 'catastrophe' has three characters and when removed and used by itself, the centre character means '**opportunity**'.

ALL of Adel's songs on her album '21' were about her catastrophic past relationships and how they drove her to desperation, depression and sadness. In fact originally, Adele was only spotted because her best friend had the presence of mind to post her music on *MySpace.*

Nevertheless, my point is that within Adele's *catastrophic* love-life was an opportunity. In this situation, the opportunity was to take all of that raw emotion and package it in a way that might touch others and might even HELP others to see that we are not alone in life's emotional roller-coaster journey and if the journey hasn't killed us... then what are the gifts lay in wait for us should we be brave enough to learn from our experience and strong enough to move on?

In some way or another everyone that we come into contact with, even for the briefest of moments, has come to assist us and us to assist them in becoming the best that we all can be. Some beautiful people do it intentionally, most people do it without even realising. For example; the tough defender on the opposing football team that makes you a quicker centre forward. The annoying nagging boss keeps you focused at all times. ***Apple*** keeps ***Microsoft*** sharp, ***Aston Martin*** keeps ***Jaguar*** pushing forward and ***Burger King*** keeps ***McDonald's*** on it's toes.

As it is with mankind so it is with man and woman on a personal level. Within every catastrophe is an opportunity for some kind of growth. The bigger the catastrophe, the bigger the potential for growth. When the source of the opportunity is acknowledged then there is a realisation that the hardship and distress were not for nothing. Certain elements of that hardship have subsequently made you an expert in the things THAT YOU NO LONGER WANT IN YOUR LIFE. And knowing what you do not want makes it easier to find what you DO WANT. You have also become a wiser more able person in the process.

All of your *'failed'* relationships were never meant to last and with all that they gave you they should not be classified as 'failures.' They came to be, in order to 'teach' you and your ex-partner, to 'prime' you and to get you ready for a relationship where you can really thrive, blossom and excel. You may be in THAT relationship now, it may be yet to come. But when it does come you will be ready because of the ***'Chinese Catastrophes'*** that occurred before... There were gifts in everyone of them. Perhaps no flowers, no chocolates and maybe no ***Aston Martin.***

But if you choose to look deep enough, you may find gifts of strength, self-preservation, endurance, will-power, positivity-in the face of negativity, cool, intelligence, inspiration, enterprise, self-belief, perhaps even resurrection. These are YOUR WELL EARNED Grammy's, the universe's daily version of Hollywood once yearly event. These are the awards for your performance that you can take with you anywhere! Once you know that you have them, you can count on them at anytime and they will work for you and get more efficient the more you use them. All that's left for me to say as I open the envelope is,

"For winning in LIFE, the Grammy goes to ... YOU!"

Now I have another written task for you and I think you can guess what it is. What "good" has come out of any of the main "wrongs" that been done to you. This could be things that you may have already touched on during meditation or even things environmental, or genetic, or things you see as fate. Nevertheless, there was a positive side to these occurrences, what were they? List them in your own shorthand style to be elaborated and analysed later. It could look something like the following example:

1) The bullying by John Smith made me take up Karate. Now I feel confident that I can protect my family. OR-

2) My mother's cooking was so bad that as a teenager I had to prepare my own food. Now I'm a top-class cook.

So we'll call these examples of positive arriving from negative, ***Chinese Catastrophe's*** and I sincerely hope I'm not offending anyone Chinese by using this term.

South African militant Steven Biko was tortured and eventually killed for his beliefs. Nelson Mandela shared the same principles and was imprisoned for over twenty-five years for his convictions. At the time of his admission on to Robin Island his wife and colleagues were undoubtedly devastated at losing yet another leader, this time to a prison sentence. But that prison sentence may have saved his life. For when he emerged more than a quarter of a century later, he found many of his former ANC comrades *had* been killed. He though, emerged at the time when his country was ready for him. He soon became South Africa's president and went on to radically change the continent as well as the mind-set of its inhabitants.

Your Personal Chinese Catastrophe's

(Good that came out of bad)

1)

2)

3)

4)

5)

6)

7)

4

Chapter 4: The Rich Thinkers Get Richer...

...While the Poor (Thinkers) **Get Poorer**

I remember waiting at a bus stop many years ago. Shortly after I arrived, a man at the wheel of a brand new Mercedes convertible drove past, roof down, with an attractive tanned blonde in the passenger seat, her hair flapping in the wind like a shampoo advert. Straightaway, a girl behind me (let's call her, Mona) said to her friend, *"Who the hell does he think he is!?"*

I wondered why the girl had to make such a comment and why is it that in our tolerant open-minded society, there are such negative reactions around displays of financial success and why wealth is often frowned upon? I also wondered if Mona realised that she was putting up a concrete wall between herself and the likelihood of her ever obtaining such a car or lifestyle, **AS WHAT YOU CRITICISE WILL NEVER BE YOUR FRIEND.** But then again perhaps she would not wish to own a posh motor vehicle and maybe she had a genuine dislike for affluence. Unfortunately however, her passionate emotional repulsion for such symbols only brought more such scenes into her life for her to view and be repulsed by. And the more she said out loud (or thought with passion) that she despised the rich; the harder her subconscious would fight (on what it thinks are ***her*** orders) to keep her poor.

Lovingly, our subconscious and intuition work tirelessly to deliver to us that which we most focus our attention on. If it's football that we place our attention on, then we will see the colours of our team in everything. And on a regular basis we will 'coincidentally' bump into others that share our passion. Likewise if you **hate** football with a passion; then you will see football wherever you go. The person you choose to have a relationship with (or a close family member-someone you are stuck forever with), will be a football fanatic and you will 'coincidentally' bump into others that **love** football regularly. This is because the subconscious mind does not differentiate between what you hate with passion and what you love with passion; all it understands is **passion.** If you complain regularly, your subconscious will think you like complaining and so give you things to complain about. If you enjoy complimenting people or praising people, it will give you an abundance of things to compliment and praise

Subsequently, the passionately voiced disgust of the bus-stop Mona, set in motion a seek-and-find operation for her subconscious and intuition. And to keep their mistress 'happy,' they continually find experiences for her where she can complain about the rich... **by maintaining** (for her) **an experience of being poor**.

And so waiting at the bus stop in South London is where she will still be found. And whatever you do... do not drive past in a convertible, as her mouth is pretty foul.

Your intuition is your own personal internal compass that guides you to your highly personalised desires, happiness and pleasures. Your subconscious mind holds the database of everything you've ever done, everything you've ever witnessed and every possible configuration of imaginable events and scenarios that could lead you to your desires, happiness and pleasures. It even works out ways to find your desires without you being consciously aware of it doing so; these moments we commonly call '*Coincidences,*' '*Chance*' or '*Luck*'.

There are some things that make you happy and there are some things that make you unhappy. And there are some things that make you **un**happy in the long-term even though you think they make you *happy* in the short-term., e.g. the wrong kind of person for a long-term relationship, the wrong job, a cash wind-fall when you're not mentally prepared for it, one last round of drinks at the bar, etc. Whatever it is, you have trained your intuition with the help of your subconscious to find whatsoever you desire and it responds most dynamically to pictures, heightened emotion (passion) and repetition.

A friend of mine has a beautiful sister who is a fashion model. Julia, is over six feet tall with an amazing figure and legs that make the *Eiffel Tower* look 'dumpy'. She regularly would complain that because she was "*... so beautiful,*" men would feel too intimidated to approach her. To the disgust of those around her she would always end the statement with, *"... I wish I was ugly!"* About eighteen months ago Julia was in a club where a fight broke out and was way too close to the action. Ultimately, two gatecrashers were eventually ejected by security men and innocent passer-by Julia, ended up with a broken nose and the loss of two front teeth, because of one wayward punch! Years of repetitively making the same emotional statement will bring the 'gift' of your request to you. I haven't seen Julia for months, but her sister tells me that she no longer says that she wishes she was ugly.

I can also remember Serge, a work colleague of mine who had the overwhelming desire to always be right. Many years ago he told me that he couldn't envisage being better than average, making more money than average or doing anything out of the ordinary because he was not fated for it. He felt that if it was his destiny to lead a better than average life, then he would have been born into it. He also tried to suggest that it wasn't worth my while investing in big plans for my own future as I would find his words to be prophetic. When I told him that his words were closer to pathetic than prophetic we had an argument there and then.

Five years later in a nightclub I managed in the Middle East, I met a flamboyant Irish millionaire named Mark and his quiet but loyal friend Jack. Silent Jack always sat ON the table, or ON the bar, NEVER on a chair, no-one ever seemed to mind.

Mark and I used to talk for hours on end, especially on Friday nights when he and Jack always showed up a little before opening time.. In the week before I left the Gulf, puffing on his big fat Cuban cigar, Mark made a statement that always stuck with me, he said,

"True wealth is a state of mind."

He continued, "*I know people who have a lot more money than I do yet they are physically, mentally and emotionally bankrupt. Take any group; say punk rockers, Hells Angels, militants, religious fanatics or any group that spend a lot of time together in the same place. They are not there because they dress alike; they are there because they think alike. Wealth is in the mind and therefore wealth is an idea. If you do not have the idea then you are not wealthy.*" He said, "*It's easier to have a lot of money than to be wealthy. That's because you do not have to be financially rich to have great wealth.Wealth is the ability to go where you want to go, or not to go anywhere if you choose not to. Wealth is the ability to be who you want to be and live your life in a manner of your own choosing. Wealth is having damn near all you want in life, which could also mean having very little in comparative terms, but that is not the issue, you have your own hearts desires and that is all that matters. Whether it comes from wealth in cash or wealth in spirit, only a truly wealthy person can live like that, and <u>you</u> my dear friend,*" he said with a great smile, "*You are very wealthy indeed!*" Ever-present Jack, sat on the table but as usual said nothing.

That particular night was a slow starter and we spoke at great length. We joked about how the richer you are the less you seem to pay for things and how often it is the ones who can most afford it, that always get free invitations for this event and that occasion, as well as expensive gifts from this person, that person and various organisations. Then Mark pointed at my chest and asked how long I'd lived in the five star Sheraton Hotel, I told him almost four years. He told me, that only a rich man could afford to do that. I said that I didn't pay as it was part of my job. His reply was to remind me of the gifts that wealthy people constantly receive and my luxurious hotel stay was one of them. <u>He</u> even remembered the time that because of a sprinkler hazard on certain floors of the hotel, I was '*forced*' to stay for some considerable time in a very special suite that had two floors, a sunken 20foot bathtub and a Jacuzzi (*ah, the things we are forced to do in life. Woe is me.) When I said that situation was pure luck, he said, "Luck my ass! **The world sees you as you project yourself.** If you think you deserve the best, even if you don't say it (in fact especially if you don't say it, but you know it), then the best will gravitate towards you. And you don't have to be mean, arrogant or aggressive; if you have 'high standards' as your friend, then high standards will enjoy following you around.*" He then said, "*One place I know* *you'll love is Monte Carlo and I know one day I'll see you there, where me you and Jack will share a long lunch in Café des Paris, watching the long-legged girls go by."* We shook hands and embraced and that was the last that I saw of him, although I did hear via mutual friends that he was still living the life of an international playboy, a sort of *James Bond* with even less morals but much more charm.

As the years passed, the universe did its' best to vividly illustrate exactly what Mark had said to me, and in the process I met an assortment of different people from right across the globe who varied in status, but all showed me the meaning of 'true' lasting wealth; wealth that was made up of more than just money. These were/are people with varying levels of financial income who manage to live life to the fullest, in ways that any observer could only describe as 'rich.'

They were different colours, religions and nationalities, male as well as female. They were different heights, sizes, facial features and some were disabled. They were all different people from an assortment of backgrounds but they did all display certain attributes that I would describe as being uniform. Those attributes are as follows:

· None were mean or 'tight' with money. *Which means instead of idolising it, they made money something they could enjoy without fear of losing it.*

· All were generous. *It was therefore easy for others to be generous towards them in return.*

· Each one seemed to understand that **what goes around comes around** and that **the best way to receive is to give**. *You cannot give what does not belong to you, whether it is a set of cutlery, lingerie, a car or absolutely anything physical or metaphysical. First you must own it before you can give it.*

· *This principle also applies to virtues and not just 'things.' You can give love, trust, faithfulness, honesty, graciousness etc, etc and the more you give, the more you will receive.*

All had vocations or jobs that they passionately enjoyed doing and would do for free! Just like my job as a DJ which, I couldn't possibly refer to as 'work,' as well as my job as a Life-Coach, which I did for free for many years.

· Each person was in some way a "humanitarian" that often gave the gift of time to those in need. Some went as far as doing charity work in the far off corners of the globe; whilst others were simply a shoulder to cry on or a compassionate ear for those who needed solace. All however, gave at the very least, some considerable thought to the plight of humanity and living things in general.

The bottom line is, **contentment is wealth**.

To be content with where you are, or where you are going in life is wealth. And just as Mark predicted, along the way I have met cash multi-millionaires and billionaires who live as if they **do not** have two pennies to rub together.

Two years after my last conversation with Mark, I received an offer to work In Monte' Carlo, hosting one of the years' most glamorous events in front of the cream of Europe's most established glitterati ***The Bal de L'Ete.'*** And for seven happy memorable years I continued to host it. Every summer my wife and I stayed in Monte Carlo's best hotels, dined in the principality's most lavish restaurants and we happily ate lunch at *Café des Paris* (all as part of my job description package). And even though we have not yet shared lunch with Mark and his good friend ***Jack*** (last name ***Daniels)***, we know that day will come. P.S. Thank you Princess Catherine Colonna de Stigliano for the organization of such a magnificent event and for my regular inclusion in that as well as the ***Bal des Etoiles*** in Paris every winter.

And while we are on the subject, I have to date bumped into an overwhelming amount of religious people in particular that are of the opinion that spirituality and the quest for a better lifestyle are incompatible. One of the main reasons for this *'impasse'* is the reference in the bible, made by Matthew 19:25, Mark 10:25 and Luke 18:25 *"It is easier for a camel to go through the eye of a needle than for a rich man to enter the kingdom of God."*

My own interpretation of this is that if an individual is rich enough to obtain absolutely anything he or she wants with little or no effort then much of the joy and appreciation can be lost in the obtaining of that goal. If an individual is always surrounded by people who never question his words or actions due to fear of losing a job, cash or perks, then how will the person in question learn and grow or know what truth dwells in the hearts of others? Can he/she ever feel unconditionally loved by anyone except family? Will he ever feel the joy of true companionship or comradeship when *perhaps* even his own wife does not see past his cash fortune?

Ultimately, glimpses of Heaven are seen through feelings like, accomplishment, sharing, selflessness, forgiveness, internal growth, compassion and of course love, etc. Unfortunately, not every rich man can get access to these things, which may mean that the view of all of Heaven may be limited for some. Likewise a poor man who treats his fellow man badly will have a similar restricted view of the Kingdom of God, no matter how skinny and underfed his camel might be!

Ultimately, I chose Mark the *Merry Millionaire's* words over the words of Serge *the Depressant*. But in effect I am (*almost*) as grateful to Serge as I am to Mark, for his words helped to mentally propel me away from that dark hopeless state of mind. In fact, to this day when I think of Serge's words I involuntarily shake my head, and when I think of what Mark said, I can't help but nod.

Again, I must say that I've never met anyone even marginally successful who hated money.

Money is like wine; it exaggerates behaviour that is already there. More of it or less of it *shouldn't* necessarily *change* an individual, although the smell of it can change the behaviour of people around you. Acquaintances and strangers in particular will tend to re-adjust themselves with the perky twitchiness of a an individual wearing an over-bleached polyester thong that's a size too small, as they try reassert their importance to you in accordance with your wealth. This quirky behaviour will take place in the event that you suddenly find yourself much richer... or much poorer.

More than 35% of lottery winners end up penniless, or worse! Because just like the dieter who has lost weight but can never see himself as being slim. A high amount of of people who get rich overnight cannot 'see' themselves as wealthy.

- William Post won $16.2m in the Pennsylvania lottery in 1988 and found himself $1m in debt one year later.
- Suzanne Mullins won $4.2m in the Virginia lottery and soon found herself $154,147.00 in debt soon after.
- John McGuiness won 10.m British Pounds in 1997 and up until recently was in debt by 2.1m.

- Evelyn Adams managed to win the New Jersey lottery TWICE in 1985 & 1986 and as I write this book she lives in a trailer park.

In order to reach or goal of a raised standard of living have you:

- ...found a job/career that you can feel passionate about to the point where you look forward to Monday mornings?
- ...gotten rid of any passed-down negative thoughts regarding the acquiring of wealth (including customised Bible quotations)?
- ...found joy in giving? (There is a difference between being generous and simply 'throwing your money away'. I never knowingly throw my money away).
- ...a passionate dislike for money or rich people? If you do, you're not helping yourself.
- ...found contentment? Is your life a reflection of your increasing contentment? Now is the time to start moving it in that direction.
- ...a sincere appreciation for what you already have? There are many things about your life that are going well. Do you see what they are and do you show signs of gratefulness? The 'universe' will always aim to give you more of what you place your passionate attention on GOOD or BAD. Try to make it the good stuff.

Expert motivational 'guru' T.Harv Eker, placed this post on Facebook in the Spring of 2012.

"Bless that which you want. If you see a person with a beautiful home, bless that person and bless that home. If you see a person with a beautiful car, bless that person and bless that car. If you see a person with a loving family, bless that person and bless that family."

5

CHAPTER 5 : MONEY/YOU ARE NOT YOUR BUSINESS CARD

(*Principle 3: **Faith***)

If you read the newspapers, watch television or listen to radio you will no doubt have heard that the world economy has been engulfed in a state of financial depression. Statements vary from, *"Two years of downturn in the real estate market,"* which I heard in June 2008, to *"The onset of a world financial horror story, the likes of which have never been witnessed by today's generation!"* I heard that last quote on the radio in August and it didn't cheer me up in the slightest. In September 2008, Alan Greenspan, Former Chairman of the U.S. Federal Reserve said without flinching,

"This is a once in a half century-probably once in a century type of event... this is in the process of outstripping anything I've ever seen and it is still not resolved and it still has a way to go." And then came October...

We've recorded the effects of stock market crashes from as recently with the 'baby crashes' of 2002, 1997 and 1970 right back to the Great Depression of 1932. We are all still shocked in 2009, yet as far back as 1802 in a letter to the then *Secretary of the Treasury*, Albert Gallatin, the **3rd President** of the United States wrote,

"I believe that banking institutions are more dangerous than standing armies. If the American people ever allow private banks to control the issue of

their currency, first by inflation then by deflation, the banks and corporations that will grow up around (the banks) will deprive the people of all property until their children wake up homeless on the continent their fathers conquered. The issuing power should be taken from the banks and restored to the people, to whom it properly belongs."

It was signed by **Thomas Jefferson** (1743-1826)

Even with history's long outstretched helpful hand we still manage to gently slide down a man-made muddy slope of mistakes individually *and* internationally in our money matters (I know I've been there!). Respected American newspaper *International Herald Tribune reported,* the IMF (*International Monetary Fund*) *"... has stated that losses stemming from the US mortgage crises might reach $1 trillion ..."* And according to **Reuters,** *"In the years since US troops went into Afghanistan to root out the al Qaeda leaders behind the September 11, 2001 attacks, spend on the conflicts totalled $2.3 trillion."* Unfortunately this forms only part of the military debt story as this atronomical figure is set to rise further as the US pays for the care of it's long-term wounded veterans, pays $1 trillion in interest payments and pays billions in costs for all manner of sundry accessories for war.

The US, Britain, the Euro-zone and most other countries around the globe are in the ongoing process of utilising a 'Fiat' (from the Latin word meaning 'Let it be so') economies to run the economies of civilisation. This means that governments can print as much money as they need to to put a sticky plaster on the broken leg of world finance. The earliest recorded use of a 'Fiat' economy was in China by the Song Dynasty in 10th Century A.D. It was used profoundly by the Roman Empire (at the time of, and just before it's fall) and in Germany at the end of WWI. I mention this because it's when a Fiat economy is used to fund war, (mankind's costliest endeavour) that the consequences of owning a printing-press and the often ensuing hyper-inflation becomes a *pressing* liability.

Now, according to Wikipedia (the extremely useful online encyclopedia-let's try to keep it), from 1944 to 1971, the *Bretton Woods* agreement fixed the value of 35 United States dollars to one troy ounce of gold. The direct link to the gold price had the benefit of keeping currencies stable. Internationally this worked perfectly as practically all major currencies world-wide were hooked up to the US dollar at fixed rates. Any trade shortfalls were easily balanced out by using the services of the IMF or international gold reserve exchanges. It was all changed by President Richard Nixon in 1971 with a decision later referred to as the 'Nixon Shock'. Since then there has been no formal link or tie of the dollar to any precious material. The present US government is using the dollar like a windscreen wiper to wash the reigns of past governments from the view of its people. But like bugs clinging on to the wiper, Sterling and the Euro still desperately grab on for dear life and shake with every movement of it's Atlantic relative. But this will be the case for as long as the dollar remains the number one default currency with which governments use to purchase oil.

If history is to be relied upon, soon, all this will lead to most governments reverting to a more stable form of economic structure, which may mean the temporary (it's never permanent) going back to pegging currency's to precious metals like gold or silver. Am I saying it would be a good idea to buy up gold and silver stock? I don't think it would be a bad idea, but in early 2012, I do think it would be rather like buying any house in 2008 at market value and expecting to make a *'killing'*. The Gold gravy train has already left the station. I do think diversification is a good idea as well as some serious overseas investment too. But **your most precious commodity is and always will be YOU**. Your creativity, your ability to change and adapt and survive.

We have now already entered into a time where how we view our world will be up for re-evaluation. So too is how we view the person we have chosen to represent us in this world... the man or woman, in the mirror.

Internationally, billions of dollars have evaporated from personal fortunes. Millions of people world-wide are losing their jobs. To many it is as if their identity has been torn away from them as you would perhaps rip a sleeve away from a worn out suit. The depression that can follow is as much for seeming loss of identity as it is for loss of income.

A sad story of 2008 involved respected English millionaire Christopher Foster, who brutally murdered his wife Jill and daughter Kirstie before setting fire to the family mansion and killing all the family pets including their dogs as well as three prize winning horses. Mr. Foster had a company called Ulva Ltd, which made insulation materials for the oil industry. Unfortunately, this business was in debt to the tune of approximately 1.8

million pounds. The family home, Osbaston House in Shropshire cost Foster 1.150m in 2004 and was being paid for via a mortgage with HSBC. Improvements to the home, which added thousands to Fosters financial woes, featured a custom-built lake, a paddock and stables. But ever so quietly he was growing more and more *un*-stable as he realised he was getting deeper and deeper into debt and closer to the prospect of losing all the material things he had acquired. To Christopher Foster, it was too much to ask for him to live without his *"business card"* his "Identity." And because he could not see a logical way out for himself, he had no reason to believe that any assistance could possibly arrive to save him from a fate that in his mind had to be worse than death, that 'embarrassing' fate was "failure."

There is a 'wealth' (for want of a better expression) of detailed assistance out there for people in financial difficulties. My personal favourite wingmen are Bill Bartmann, Brendon Burchard, Darren Hardy (Success Magazine), Robert Kiyosaki and Anthony Robbins all of which offer revolutionary perspectives on achieving and maintaining great wealth, from below zero, right up to stratospheric levels.

Chris Foster believed he was a 'failure' and in his mind his downward spiral of desperation could not possibly be reversed. In the following chapter we will take a look at some other *'failures'* for a moment, to see if perhaps Foster's self-assessment may have been unfairly pre-mature...

"If laid out end to end, the brain cells of just one human being,
Would stretch across the British Isles from Lands End to Scotland,
Ah, bonny Scotland,
And during our everyday lives,
We cleverly manage to use no more than the area of say... London.
Good old London.
We hold a bottle that contains four pints,
But we drink less than a quarter of its' production,
We've been given a book the size of Chekov's War and Peace,
But we never get past the introduction.

We have been given a road map the size of the universe,
Which states every street, in every city, in every country,
On every planet,
And it does it...
In a manner most clear,
But we never make it past the little arrow,
That politely states... "You are here."
That's because we are taught the ungodly,
And we're programmed to accept always less.
We believe in our peers unquestionably,
And we pay too much homage to television sets.
Cable, satellite channels one to one hundred and three.
Few ever go deeper than a one-inch man-made screen.
There are just so many unworthy influences,
That we load with undue esteem.
Yet the light of the spirit which carries us,
Does not even get a look in."

6

Chapter 6: If You've been made made to Feel Like a Failure

(...Then You are Very Special Indeed)

Dear readerIf*you've been made to feel like a failure**, it turns out that you are in esteemed company... Unsigned and unknown, a 17 year-old **George Michael** had his tape of *Careless Whisper*, physically thrown back at him with the record company executive saying abruptly, *"You've learned how to sing, now go away and learn how to write a good song*!" **J. K Rowling'sHarry Potter & the Philosopher's Stone* was rejected by 12 different publishers before it was finally taken on by *BloomsburyPress.* The parents of pupils at **Jesse J's** primary school complained so much about Jesse's voice being loud that she was ejected from the school choir.

Scores of famous people have 'failed' in their money-matters many have even been bankrupt. I will list just a few: **Bjorn Borg** (Tennis Player), **Kim Basinger** (Actress), **Al Jolson** (Singer), **Abraham Lincoln** (16th President of the USA), **Meatloaf** (Singer), **Charles Goodyear** (Tyre inventor), **Rembrandt** (Painter) etc, etc.

In 1998 soul singer **Toni Braxton**, was bankrupt to the tune of $3.9 million and had to sell her Awards and household possessions to cover her debt. But, by the end of 1999 she signed a new recording contract worth $25 million. Boxer **George Foreman**'s bankruptcy took him back into the ring in 1994 at the sprightly age of 45. Foreman beat Michael Moorer to regain the title he first held twenty years prior. The win increased his celebrity status and greatly assisted his entrepreneurial ventures, putting him *literally* back on the gravy train in earnest. Film director **Francis Ford Copolla** was bankrupt by -$300,000.00 BEFORE the **FIRST***Godfather* movie. **Henry Ford's**first car company (*Detroit Automobile Company*) went bankrupt in 1901 and a year later his second company, the *Henry Ford Company* also miserably ran out of gas, . Before he reached Hollywood, **Walt Disney** went bankrupt in 1921; ***Mickey Mouse* however, made his screen debut in 1928. Donald Trump** went bankrupt in the early nineties (the decade, NOT his age) by a towering undisclosed figure totalling hundreds of millions of dollars. Nevertheless, he managed to *trump* that in 2004 when he went bankrupt to the fanfare requiring tune of **$1.8 billion!** Nominated for his role in Chaplin but no amount of laughter could cover up the mess that Robert Downey Jr. was also in during the 1990's. His heavy drug habit had lost him friends, work and money. He begged Larry Hagman for cash but Hagman said he'd rather pay for Robert's rehab. In 1996, he was pulled-over by Malibu Law Enforcement who searched his car and found a gun, cocaine, heroin and crack. One night Downey was so intoxicated he stumbled into a stranger's home and fell asleep in the bed of an 11-year-old. Sean Penn physically flew Downey out of state to get him into rehab. Unfortunately he was out in 24 hours back on his road to potential self-destruction.

The point of significance regarding all of the above, is that they all went on to make their indelible mark on society **or further** laid their stake to fame **after they were made to feel like failures either by themselves or by those whose opinions they respected.**

In other words, had the individuals highlighted above committed suicide or given up on their dreams when they felt they had failed, then we would not have had: *Harry Potter, Careless Whisper,The Godfather Trilogy,* the *Ford Mustang,Mickey, Minnie, Pluto, Donald* or *Goofy,The Apprentice,*

Price Tag, Iron-Man (Robert Downey Jr. style), theGeorge Foreman Grill and the *George Foreman 12205 Next Generation Grill* with (I hasten to add) removable plates!

The best part of all of this is that you don't have to be an aspiring singer, film-maker or actor. You might just want to be a better mother or a better father; a better husband or wife or partner. You might be giving up drugs or alcohol, hurting yourself or others. You're not a failure because you haven't made it BIG! You're special to someone my friend! You don't have to be running for the United States Presidency. You could be running (or jogging) for a better state of health. You may not wish to be the richest man on Earth; you may simply seek employment or a promotion. You may not want to gain weight for a title fight. You may want to lose weight for your wedding. You may not want to write a best-seller. You may want to right a few wrongs and put your life back in order. In summary, you may simply wish to be **the best possible you...** And there's nothing wrong with that! But it may not be easy.

Those listed above are made of the same flesh and blood as you and I. **George Michael** knew *Careless Whisper* was special and he didn't give up on his creation or his passion. Years later he saw the same executive at an awards ceremony and took great pleasure in re-introducing himself and his award winning legendary song that had sold more than six-million copies worldwide!

Your creations are extensions of who you are; your ideas/ your children/ your passions/YOUR VISION OF WHAT YOUR DESTINY LOOKS LIKE...**NEVER GIVE UP ON THEM.** The entire world does not necessarily have to see all you have created. The woman who every year lovingly tends to the blossoming flowers in her window box, will not have less pride and satisfaction than a designer at the Chelsea Flower Show. And if an unexpected storm should arrive, both will have to start again... from zero.

D**o not** assume the universe has given up on you whilst you are being **tested** to show how robust is your resolve for success. **HAVE FAITH.** Often your willpower will be questioned. You may face ridicule. You may be laughed at, derided, distracted. And you WILL make mistakes, some HUGE *(I made another one today!).* That's all part of the build-up towards the unimaginable feelings of ELATION and accomplishment you will have when you reach your destination! Give your guided eternal spirit a chance. **You do not know what you are truly capable of.** Ask yourself this vital question,

"Is this something I could do even if I wasn't getting paid for it?"

Answer yourself honestly. The world holds its breath as you make up your mind and the universe masses its goodwill armies along the border exclusively on your behalf waiting for your answer, waiting for the perfect time. **THEN** when you are clear where your **passion** lies... Innumerable bombs of inspiration will clear the way before you. Rockets of motivation will send you further than you thought you could fly. And all around will benefit from the positive effects of the radiation your momentum will create.

You have not failed, far from it. It didn't seem to work out for you on this particular occasion. Or maybe you have to approach the object of your desire from a different physical or mental attitude. Take some time for tears and self-pity (sometimes we all need a little bit of that). You have gained a better insight into what exactly you are dealing with. When you move forward now you will not do so alone. **Now pick yourself back up and get on with it! Starting TODAY! Have Faith. You have a destiny to fulfil.**

- **Have Faith in the FACT that a happy life filled with meaning is your birthright.**
- **Your impending successes will be made all the more sweeter by your personal history of challenges.**
- **Start your Faith *'ball'* rolling by understanding that whatever your conditions, you are alive with complete dominion over your own thoughts and therefore you have the power to imagine your existence at least 1 percent better than what it might be now; this a thought process that you can repeat over and over and over again until it becomes reality.**

- **Although you should have Faith in yourself; having Faith in an omnipresent omnipotent force stronger and wiser than you, that may be able to guide and assist you will increase exponentially your capability to attract all manner of goodness and *even* miracles regularly into your life. One does not need to be '*religious*' to believe this. In fact one can even believe in God without being religious if one so chooses.**
- **Faith means being happy. If you know things will turn out right in the end, you then have no need to be sad or depressed. Nevertheless, no one can be a permanent beach-ball throwing, candy floss munching, Cum-by-Yah-My-Lord singing, happy little bunny! We get illnesses, bills need to be paid and there's that thing about loss and death that can put a dark cloud over your afternoon. What I'm talking about is the general spirit in how we flavour our day. Being happy is a choice, an election, a decision; choose happiness. This decision is much easier once you have chosen to have Faith.**
- **Faith means seeing the learning opportunity in all experiences, no matter how challenging the experience.**

7

Chapter 7. Sexual Energy

(.. It's what you do with with it that counts)

There is a form of energy that is so potent that it can cause presidents and politicians to lose track and indeed lose elections. Unchecked, this form of energy can put a man in prison and give a woman a feeling of self-shame that can remain with her for life. In a way this powerful force is the number one reason why the human race continues to exist and why as long as we have a planet to live on, we will have new generations to fill it. The energy in question is SEXUAL ENERGY; we all have it, but there is more than one reason why.

There is nothing wrong with having a strong sex drive. If you look at some of the most successful individuals throughout history, in more cases than not, a robust appetite for sex, features in most CV's (I don't mean that literally). From Napoleon, to Alexander the Great, from Henry VIII to John F. Kennedy, from Michael Jordan to Ryan Giggs; success on any scale is the greatest of all aphrodisiacs. Power, wealth *and* success blended together is almost too sexy a mix for a soul to bear.

In most cases for most people, regular great sex can only happen if there are corressponding long periods without mental worry. In other words, long periods without financial stresses or major health concerns.

Consequently, teenagers and those in their early twenties who have not yet racked up credit large card bills, loans or mortgages will automatically find their minds free enough from anxiety to get an erection even from the slightest change of wind direction. And every other week a girl will 'fall in love' (some would say fall in *lust)* with a new teen heart-throb. Mother nature also plays a part, ensuring that during our healthiest optimum child-bearing years we are topped up with so much estrogen and so much testosterone that we are like walking champagne bottles rigorously shaken-up about to spray the entire village as if every night was New Year's Eve!

As you exit your twenties, a strange phenomenon begins to consume your being (well, your mind at least); it's called **intelligence.** Intelligence makes only fleetingly brief appearances before 25. It's like the trailer that you see for the movie that will hit the screens for women <u>usually</u> after age 30 and for most men not until well past 40! And this is because sex is highly distracting. Being fertile with fully working parts is a tough challenge to hold down.

Outspoken social commentator, comedian and atheist, Bill Maher said the following in a recent CNN interview on the Piers Morgan Tonight show,

" I say what I feel and that will piss a lot of people off! But they can't say I'm a liar, and to me not getting married was part of that. Now some people just have a very strong libido and you just have to deal with it. And if I had gotten married, anytime before now I couldn't have been faithful. So I just live the life where I could be true to myself AND true to other people. People have very different libido levels. Some people are just hornier! ... I found it subsided a bit after I turned 50, or in my early fifties and it was a great relief, it was like getting a monkey off your back."

This is one of the reasons why when you decide to settle down, you should do it with someone you find sexually attractive in both a physical *and* mental way. Otherwise, you will be ever-so easily be 'distracted' away from your course to **the best possible you**. How much has Tiger Woods game suffered? How much did Bill Clinton's career suffer? How much has

Arnold Schwarzenegger's future political prospects suffered? And what bank will employ (Sir) Fred Goodwin?

We all have a sexual animal that lurks beneath the camouflage of our everyday guises, but assuming sexual energy is exclusively for sex, is like assuming cash is exclusively for placing inside your wallet-and nothing else! That's why most sports coaches ask their players not to have sex the night before a game. Clever individuals who know about sexual energy, know that utilising it properly will give you the edge in **ANY** competition, **any** trial, **any** pursuit and **any** challenge. Don't waste this precious in-built-emergency-booster-pack on a meaningless fling.

Talk to your partner about who you really are and what things really set your heart racing. BE HONEST NOW! Being honest in the future might be too late. You never know, you might get the surprise of your life when your partner turns around and says, "***You are a very naughty person indeed!*** *I thought I was the only one who had those kind of thoughts... Let's talk more about this upstairs...*"
Then you will have all of the full range of services in-house that you thought you had to go outside to find.

I am not a sex therapist. My passion is to help individuals reach their potential and experience their destiny in it's fullest and most grand way. But so often, this great potential is curtailed and a shining destiny destroyed, because of a needless fling, a one night stand, an extra-marital affair, etc, etc, even though the amount of attention, time and money needed to start an affair is more than the amount needed to maintain a current (good) relationship.

A supportive loving relationship will add years to your life, fill you with well-being and help you reach dizzy heights of achievement in all fields. A bad relationship is a parasitic and draining. Both partners have a part to play. Even in times of great stress, maintain constant honest dialogue and keep nothing hidden. No one should need to find 'someone else' to share problems with. Share your dreams, hopes, fears and sexual fantasies with each other. You may just stumble upon a huge treasure chest you never realised you had! Everyday be thankful for your partner and all the things he/she brings to your life. Let your partner know how special he/she is, as often as possible. Every few months or so have a game of **five things you like** and

one thing you don't like about each other. It can be a tricky game but if done with love, compassion, diplomacy and humour it can be an ego boost as well as informative and fun. Intuitively, you chose each other for a reason or many reasons. Now enjoy the journey of finding out what those reasons are.

Gentlemen in particular; do not sexually underestimate the woman living under the same roof as you. If you give her the chance she can turn your world right round. So give her the chance. Make her your queen and she will make you king of all that your eyes can see. She may also have one or two things she'd like to share with you too; so come to the table with an open mind and listen as well as speak.

Ladies, men were born with muscles and not a great deal more. You were born with less muscles, but you have hips and you have the larger share of INTUITION! You have more intuition in your little finger than most men have in a football stadium filled with men who have all their fingers. You know who is right for you and you know who is wrong right at the outset. Often you choose who is wrong for the fun of it, and then you admit later that **you knew all along** that it he was wrong! In the meantime, unless you are a teenager you lose time. Yes, you can change some; you can change a lion into a purring cat but you can't change an alligator into mouse so don't bother trying. You don't need to try.

You are the center of the universe. **Marc Anthony** and **Julius Caesar** almost gave up the expansive kingdom of Rome for **Cleopatra.King Edward VIII** abdicated from the throne and turned his back on the British Empire for **Wallis Simpson** who was a married American already once **divorced.King Akenaton** of Egypt changed the religion of an entire civilisation for his wife **Nefertiti,** and the legendary city of ancient Troy was destroyed by **King Menelaus** in order to bring his wife **Helen of Troy** back to Sparta (and that was already the SECOND time she was 'abducted' by another infatuated man!).

(You who call yourselves women; be sure this world remains in balance because it revolves around YOU. Just don't tell any man that you know this, or you'll give the game away.)

It's time you understood, without embarrassment... Your power is immense and sexual energy forms part of that power. Put another way, scientifically speaking; testosterone is **the** 'sex' hormone and men have more of it. But who has more POWER, the aggressive pollen-hunting male Worker bees or the calculating living-the-life-of luxury well-fed Queen bee? It's how you use what you have that counts.

8

Chapter 8: Potential is Everywhere All the Time

(*Principle* 4: Readiness)

If when you get lemons you make lemonade, what happens when you get bad hair days?

Because you have not yet mastered the art of reading the future and because you may have not yet come to terms with true open-mindedness; to compensate you must try your best to be in a constant state of *Readiness.* The opportunity to change your fate can arrive and depart in a moment more fleeting than the change of British weather in summertime. Here (London, UK) *we can literally experience what feels like all four seasons in one day. Most briefcases and handbags feature a fold-up rain coat, an umbrella, sunglasses and a small bottle of water in case of dehydration.*

The obvious stuff first: Be as healthy and as fit as you can possibly be at all times (e.g. Yoga and a weight-bearing activity). In your chosen fields, remain as knowledgeable and up to date as possible. Remain as sober and as clear headed as you can. Meditate as often as you can.

Getting ahead is often about spotting an opportunity before the next man has wiped the sleep out of his eyes.

When the world is reeling from a global catastrophe, most people are in readiness for more bad news. I'm asking you to put yourself in readiness for the good news lurking beneath. Potential doesn't only abide within catastrophe's... **Potential is everywhere all the time,** but often undetectable to the naked eye. With faith, imagination, intuition and open-mindedness the potential in every situation begins to sparkle like camera flashes at a pop concert. Being in a state of readiness means you are less likely to miss an opportunity when it arrives.

Don't complain about not fitting into a wedding dress when you knew a year ago the date of your wedding. Don't say you were not prepared for the job interview when you have all the necessary literature at home or available to you on the internet.

If you are the victim of abuse, your bags can be packed and ready; your abuser will have to leave the house at some point, when opportunity flashes before your eyes, make sure you are in a state of readiness.

All movement towards a state of readiness alerts the universe-at-large of your sincere impassioned intentions. If these intentions are in line with the higher good, you can be sure a way toward your goal will be illuminated for you. But be open-minded, your way outward or upward may not look like what you have envisioned.

Please consider the story of another survivor and hero, her name was Sarah.

During her early years, African-American Sarah Breedlove, known in later life as Madame C.J. Walker, lived a life that **no one** living in today's world would envy. She was born in Delta, Louisiana, USA in 1867. She had two brothers and an older sister. In a bid to escape the deadly *Yellow Fever* epidemic that had claimed her parents and was running rampant through that part of the US, Sarah and sister Louvenia fled to Vicksburg, where they also hoped they would find employment as maids.

Soon, Louvenia was married and Sarah, too young to fend for herself remained living with her sister and new husband. Unfortunately, Louvenia's spouse was physically abusive to both girls and Sarah desperately needed a way out. At the tender age of just **fourteen** she spotted a route that she felt she *had* to take... She married a man named Moses McWilliams and they had a beautiful, bright-eyed daughter they named Leila. But before Leila reached her third birthday, her father was brutally murdered, which left Sarah a twenty-two year-old widow and single parent.

At age twenty-six Sarah married again, this time to a man named John Davis. It was a tempestuous emotionally draining marriage that lasted ten years.

Having had enough, Sarah then decided to make a clean break of it and moved to St. Louis, where she hoped she and her daughter could have a fresh start at life. There, for work she cleaned and ironed clothes every day and studied hard at night-school most evenings.

Somehow this feisty woman never allowed her own optimism or self-esteem to deflate or disappear. Even with a drastic lack of funds and a hectic schedule of school, work and taking care of her beloved daughter, she never allowed her appearance to be anything less than pristine and presentable at all times. But being so very busy and looking so very good can be a challenge even for a 21st Century woman, try to imagine how it must have been for a poor, single African-American mother living in the USA over one hundred years ago. Sarah had to think of a way to save precious time, do all the things she needed to do and yet somehow maintain her appearance in a fiercely competitive new age . So by way of '*necessity*', Sarah created a beautifying hair-straightening system that cut down her preparation time and gave her a look she found physically enhancing. She had a notion that other African-American women would also find her invention useful. She was right, and soon her new creation became a profitable business.

In completely unchartered business territory Sarah relocated, this time to Denver where she met the charming Charles Joseph Walker. She rolled the dice of love yet again and threw them *as well as* 'caution' to the wind and married Walker in the winter of 1906. They travelled the length of the country setting up offices and promoting the newly formed ***Madame C.J. Walker*** products and brand name. In 1910, the marriage unfortunately ended, but all aspects of the business continued to boom. Eventually she had more than one thousand employees working directly under her, these were known as *Walkers Agents,* she had a college in Pittsburgh called the *Leila College for Walker Hair Culturists* and business head-quarters in Indianapolis and New York.

At a time when an entire nation was still trying to recover from trying to enslave itself and the true identity of a country, a government and its people was being painfully forged into pages of history as well as the psyche of it's inhabitants. At this pivotal moment in time it's highly *likely* that a proud single mother said to herself,

"I'm just so fed up with bad hair days."

Passionate Sarah Breedlove, otherwise known as C.J. Walker went on to become the Nations first African-American Millionaire. She died in 1919 and left behind a thriving business, a wealthy daughter and an awesome thirty-four room mansion built on the banks of the Hudson River.

Just so **you** wouldn't have to be the first, countless others have risked everything to prove to **you** dear reader, that neither race, background, education, being rich, being poor or *Other People's Logic* can decide **your** destiny for **you.** Throughout this book I will return often to this point. Put another way,

"If you dream as big as you can dream, anything is possible, no matter what you set your imagination to, anything can happen."

The above quote was said with passion in Beijing by the worlds greatest ever Olympian, Michael Phelps, who won 8 gold medals at the 08.08.2008 Olympic games.

Dear reader, even at this very moment there are opportunities to become the best possible you that are like the rays of early spring sunshine darting in at angles through wooden blinds in the attempt to signify the oncoming change of season. That's because every time a 'reverse' trend, *collapse* or *bust* occurs you can bet your last penny there are many still profiting and profiting well from the situation.

As an illustration, as I write this particular piece, 2009 hasn't yet come to it's end and already I've read about David Tepper, an American hedge fund manager for *Appaloosa Management,* who bet that the US banks would rally with gusto to slow down the depression. As the screaming villagers started heading for the hills in panic, David bought a colossal amount of shares in *Bank of America* and *Citibank.* He says, *"I felt like I was alone, no one was even bidding."*

David rubs his testicles for luck. I'm serious; he keeps a pair of oversize brass testicles on his desk, which he apparently rubs when he needs good fortune.

Ultimately, the government's first bank rescue package ensured his fund grew by 120%, netting *Appaloosa Management,* 4.4 billion pounds in profit, with Tepper hauling in a useful 1.56 billion pounds personal payout for his readiness and **intuitive** efforts, which, came just in time for Christmas. Nice.

One of the main objectives of *The Best Possible You* is to make you rich, much richer than your present dreams might allow. And richer in ways that may or may not include money. But, do not be tempted to assume this book is solely for out-of-work bankers. It is for **anyone**, in any profession, working or unemployed who believes he/she has more to give to a world that knows very little about him/her. And it is for the person who believes the world has something to give to him/her in return. It is for those who involuntarily find themselves spinning uncontrollably in this vortex of *change* and its' for those who voluntarily want to start the process of *change* for themselves.

I call it *change*. Others may call it *loss*, or *demotion* or *redundancy* or other things like *"Stock Market collapse," "Knock-on -effect"* and *"Drop in share prices" etc.* It is still change. At close range the situation looks and *is* very sad, and can be very depressing. But with the luxury of time, a long time for some or a moment if you so direct your mind, it can be seen simply as *change.*

In addition, this book is not just about work. The same principles apply each time a divorce happens, as it potentially puts another eligible single person back into circulation, every time a car leaves a parking bay it's made vacant for the next car. The dazzling array of the myriad rainbow colours painted on autumn leaves are made available solely through summer's sad exit. And every day the sun goes down… only to make way for the dramatic entrance of a glorious romantic moon… the view of which, is often blocked by *dark clouds*. And so I sincerely ask you. What beauty, what glory is missing from your life because of your '*clouds*'? The moon and the sun **do not** evaporate into nothingness just because you can't see them. They are still hard at work doing what we love them doing, providing warmth, light and the perfect amount of gravitational pull to keep your underwear from detaching and floating off into outer space as well as other *more* or *less* important things.

So then we have to admit there are things which we cannot see, like gravity, that still manage to assist us in the most grand of ways. And on a daily basis things may be going **right,** at the precise time that we may be completely **convinced** they are going horribly wrong. When it's impossible to see or hear or even touch what you need to assist you in a given situation, you then have to rely on **intuition** and the ability to look past the obvious, to locate the **truth** about your joy and happiness that resolutely lies beneath.

- Prospering (like David Tepper) instead of sinking is using your *intuition* instead of your sight and being **open-minded** about the situation at hand.
- You help no-one by proving bad luck, sickness or poverty are contagious, they are not! It's not what you've done or what you see that determines your destiny; it's not even about your history ref: C. J. Walker. It's what you constantly think and do that will map out your future!
- Your wellness, prosperity and success in any area is not based on others who have tried what you intend to do. Do not compare yourself to others.
- Within two years I've twice received litigation/repossession papers from my bank. In the same time two companies I worked for went into sudden liquidation. And still during the very same period, my 94 year old grandmother lost all sense of reality, became totally bed-bound and passed away and my mother was diagnosed with breast-cancer. Using my intuition and having faith would have been impossible if I focused on only what I saw around me. I knew there was a way out for me and my family and I never gave up. My mother's treatment has been 100% successful, we didn't lose our home and now I earn more than ever. And that's because I used my surplus free time to finish my book!
- Other people's failures are not provided to teach you that a thing cannot be done. They are provided to teach you a thing cannot be done a particular way by a particular person.
- No matter how dire the situation; no matter how desperate; a way of not just survival, but a way of success has been already supplied. You just have to find it.
- Choose more often with your heart.

- Neither colour, poverty; not even physical disabilities should be seen chains to hold you back. They are springboards for your unique story of hope and encouragement for everyone.
- Your dreams may be just about to happen: Be as fit as you can be, be as focused as you can be, be as organised as you can be. BE READY!
- Sight can be distracting.

9

Chapter 9: Why Your 'Enemy' is Sometimes Your Best Friend

Whilst doing my DJ work I often get asked for out-of-the-blue random songs that can potentially disrupt the flow of the evening and cast to the wind any form of system or planning that I might have set up. I never say no, I always say, *"Let me check to see if I've brought it."* This gives me time to think of the best possible moment to play the song. I also need to asses what song(s) will be the musical '*bridge*' that I can put in, to go from Underground House music (for example), to Frank Sinatra? What can I use to lead my audience from Hip-Hop to the Rolling Stones and then back to Hip Hop again, without being pelted with rotten fruit and tomatoes by the remaining 99% of the gathering? There is always an answer, there is ALWAYS a way. I just have to find it. The applause at the end of a night makes me FEEL great, but it's answering the challenges throughout the night that make a DJ great enough to earn that applause. My audiences have always been mixed in age and nationality and if you ask me for a song with a smile you are guaranteed to get it and quickly (non-smiling people will still get their requests, just not as fast).

Every difficult request has stretched me as a DJ. I was the first non-Arabic DJ to play Arabic music in a London Club in 1985. I was the first non-Russian to play Russian Music in a London club in 1997. In Monte Carlo and Paris I regularly played classic Waltz.

Most DJ's do not accept requests as it obliterates their playlist. They tend to see the person asking for the request almost as 'the enemy,' someone whose sole objective is to ruin their night! My reputation has been ***built*** on entertaining and 'educating' a crowd simultaneously and never refusing a request.

I've always been willing to forsake looking like a *'cool'* DJ that only plays only the trendiest songs. Instead, I've taken chances every night in the pursuit of making people not just happy, but ecstatic! This living outside my comfort zone has eventually led to me being treated like a mini pop star. I've been in countless private jets, helicopters and 5-Star hotels. I've also had private chauffeurs assigned to me for the full weekend of my assignments as well as Mercedes and Rolls Royces meeting me and my wife at the airport (whenever possible I bring my wife to events). All this and more because I consistently take up the challenge of doing a little extra to make someone's night (sometimes through gritted teeth). All this because I choose not to see a 'request' as an insult. **All this because no matter how challenging, I know there is always a way.** I know that before a question is asked, an answer has already been given… We just have to find it. The enemy is not the difficult customer who seems to be trying to ruin the evening by telling me what he thinks I can do. **The enemy is the voice within me that says what it thinks I cannot do.**

Do not run away from what is being asked of you in any circumstance, work or leisure. At least have a think about it and try to be open-minded. You have no idea where it might take you.

No one is here to pull you down; everyone around you has been sent to only lift you up… That is whether they know it or not, whether they intend to or not, whether it looks that way or not (remember, sight can be distracting), or whether you think it is or not.

In the American version of *Strictly Come Dancing*, called, *Dancing with the Stars*, Donny Osmond said *"I want to win this mirror ball so badly because if you had a sister named Marie and she was going to rub it in your face for the rest of your life. You would want to win it too."* Donny Osmond won.

And on the eve of the BBC's *Strictly Come Dancing* semi-final 2009; sports commentator Chris Hollins, son of Chelsea legend John Hollins, spoke of Ola Jordan, his professional partner and summarised his performance to date:

"Every week for the past 13 weeks before we go out to dance, she says, 'I believe in you, I believe in you, I believe in you.' For the very first time, I actually believe in my self, and that's all down to Ola." Chris Hollins, the only contestant to have never been in the show's 'dance-off,' went straight through to the final and won.

Half of England is often struck speechless whenever Sir Alex Ferguson leaves certain key players out of his Manchester United squad, especially for important matches and I would imagine that the unselected individuals might feel victimised. But the manager knows the heart and immense pride of his players. This is why he acquired them in the first place. He also knows that on the given signal they are likely to react like a rabid Doberman dogs given the scent of the goal and hungrily devour every inch of the pitch on their way. Sir Alex will hold back until he alone thinks it is the right time to let his thoroughbreds out of the stocks. In the meantime the whole team may feel the length of his sword-like tongue.

Ex- United star Mark Hughes, often called Ferguson *"The Hairdryer,"* because he would scold his players straight after the game in the dressing room and anyone that played particularly badly would be ferociously shouted at from less than an inch away, face to face. Hughes said that Sir Alex had often cornered him while he was still dripping wet from the shower and the sheer velocity of the ensuing verbal abuse left his hair blow-dried into a style similar to riding a motorbike without a crash helmet at very high speed. Under Sir Alex Fergusson's reign, Manchester United have amassed more trophies than any other British football club in History.

Dear Reader, have a serious think about the people that constantly annoy you in your life. I will NOT ask you to write their names down (you never know who's looking over your shoulder). But I will ask you to analyze the part of your character they have managed to ENHANCE. I have a friend (we'll call Lola) who get's wound up by a young ultra-efficient secretary that joined her office within the last six-months. Lola has complained that because she doesn't want to look bad next to this 'upstart' she has had to 'polish' her presentations more than she needed to six moths ago. In addition Lola says she is stressed from having to actually 'learn' things rather than '*blagging,*' as she was scared the new secretary might expose Lola's flaws at the new regular staff meetings that she has 'efficiently' set-up. In a panic, Lola was set to leave, but management had noticed a sharp upturn in the quality of Lola's work and asked her to stay, almost <u>doubling</u> her salary in the process. Lola was over the moon! But if it wasn't for the sassy pushy new secretary, there would have been every chance that instead of a raise, Lola, in time, could have been fired.

So think about who you dislike or find irritating. Think of why you dislike this person. Think of what actions you have had to take to deal with having this person in your life. Ask yourself sincerely if the sudden update of your own skills or personality may help you handle your life and the outside world better?

There are some exceptions, but in 9 cases out of 10, you will find, ***Your Enemy is Sometimes Your Best Friend.***

10

Chapter 10: Take Control and Watch out for O.P.L

O.P.L. (Other Peoples Logic)
It could burn your hair off

How often have you said or done something in regretful error that was based on what you were told or even ordered to do by someone you felt was an authority on that particular subject. Your mother, father, teacher, brother, sister, boss, friend, television programs; intuitively we know who and what we should be listening to.

We risk more than just losing face when we continually assign ***Other People'slogic*** to be our life's only decision maker. For instance, before Greek Philosopher Aristotle (384-322 BC) arrived, everyone on Earth thought that logic stated the world to be flat! Believe it or not, in 1890's America, "scientific" results showed that **too mucheducation** could seriously damage the female reproductive organs! And in 1905, former President Grover Cleveland, eloquently stated his views in an interview for a women's magazine (*Ladies Home Journal*) saying that women having the right to vote would upset *"A natural equilibrium so nicely adjusted to the attributes and limitations of both (men and women) that it cannot be disturbed without social confusion and peril."*

Is it possible that the logic of a United States president could be so far removed from reality?

If you think seriously about it for a moment you'll see most *"logic"* is simply someone else's fence around their own **comfort-zone** that very inconveniently encroaches into ***your*** space/***your*** zone. **O.P.L** is a set of rules that **primarily** work for someone else. A welcome consequence is that ***it can also work for you***... even if you didn't invent it, just like the idea of the motor-car, the telephone or the internet. These and millions of other such ideas enhance the quality of life of those who believe in them. If an idea does not enhance the quality of your life, perhaps you should question it. For example all of the *'isms'* such as racism, ageism, sexism, terrorism do not enhance the quality of life on Earth.

Dear reader this manual may represent your greatest opportunity to escape *Other Peoples Logic* to live a fearless life that is in synchronisation with the actual truth about who you really are. **The sheer power in having *Faith* in a brighter destiny for yourself and your loved ones cannot be underestimated.** The art of following heart is not an effortless vocation. The willingness to stand up to naysayers comes at a price: Embarrassment, mild or major ridicule, or some financial loss is usually what you may be faced with at the very beginning. And although those negative aspects do not last forever... while it is happening, it most certainly feels as if it will never end. Read again Chapter 5. Faith is key to your survival and future success.

Follow your *intuition* with *intention* along the path laid down by your *imagination.* Your *faith* will sometimes falter, but never let it die.

Shakira Isabel Mebarak Ripoll, fans of full-blooded-earthy Latin music know her simply by first name, Shakira, was refused entry into her school choir whilst in second grade. Her music teacher informed her that her vibrato was too low and a chorus of classmates took joy in saying her voice sounded like the "...bleating of a goat." However since her school days, Shakira has become Latin music's hottest global talent. Her albums are multi-million sellers, with *"Laundry Service,"* selling over twenty-million copies and still counting. In addition, her massive duet with Wyclef Jean, *"Hips Don't Lie,"* is one of the most successful singles of the 21st Century!

The world's richest man (2008) Warren Buffet, was refused a place at Harvard Business School. Even though he had displayed a practical aptitude for business since the age of six! Nevertheless, Harvard rejected him in what is regarded as the worst admission decision in their history. By way of the perfect example, Harvard's loss is your gain. **For even when the world seems perfectly qualified to shout at you many things; it can never tell you what you can be. That choice belongs only to you.** Your finely tuned intuition can guide you to who or what you should be listening to, or in fact if you should even be listening at all!

Let's be clear on this; I'm not suggesting that it is your task to change the world. I'm not even asking you to change your socks. **At this point** what I'm asking needs no outward action from you whatsoever. **At this point** all I'm asking is that you consider changing how you see yourself. Don't do anything just yet, simply ponder the thought for a moment and then ask yourself if you feel that you are as happy as you could possibly be at present? Is your life positively delivering to you all that you would require of it to make you happy? For if you are perfectly content with your lot in life, then this book may not even be for you. However, if you think there may be more for you to give and certainly more for you to receive at home and perhaps in the world at large, then read on. Right now all I'm asking is that you appreciate there is more to **you** than what you may have considered up to this point... MUCH, MUCH, MUCH, MORE.

The teachings of our society mean that there are many whose words and actions we do not question, words and actions we are programmed to believe unconditionally. People such as parents, religious leaders, teachers, government officials, doctors...

Dear reader you have a source of information of your own that is **never** wrong and is more knowledgeable than those we placed blindly upon a the unapproachable pedestal... in most cases without justification. Our loving parents in particular honestly believe hand-on-heart that they have only your own best interests in mind when they persuade you to be or do things against your own wishes...

In September 1983, quietly spoken, Katherine Esther Jackson beloved by all of her children, begged her son the undisputed King of Pop, Michael Joseph Jackson, to join his brothers on their last ever tour as the

Jacksons. The tour was called *The Victory Tour.* Up until his mothers' personal request Michael had refused the invitation, with his *Off The Wall* and *Thriller* albums, he had already established himself as a solo artist without equal and in June of 1983 he successfully fired his father Joe from his job as manager and was now whole-heartedly enjoying his well earned independence and new creative freedom. In fact there were many aspects of the impending *Victory Tour* that Michael did not like, including the Post Office only/bulk-order-only way the fans had to purchase their tickets. This, along with father Joe's managerial involvement made the tour a very unattractive prospect for the rising star and only dear mother Katherine, could persuade her son to perform with his siblings. (At this point I have to strongly state that it ***is*** a parents' duty to look after all of his/her children in the best possible way he/she knows how) Katherine did what any loving mother in the same circumstance would have done. She **undoubtedly** most sincerely wanted what she thought was best for all of her family. And the fact that Michael named her in his will as the legal guardian of his three children states unequivocally the unlimited faith and trust he had in his mother.

Drinks giant *Pepsi* soon became involved with the tour and on 27th January 1984 a lighting effect exploded on set during the filming of a *Pepsi* commercial as Michael sang *Billie Jean* in front of three thousand screaming fans. With his brothers rushing to his aid, Michael's hair caught fire and his scalp needed treatment for the resulting 2nd degree burns. From then on Michael became addicted to prescription drugs and pain-killers. The course of his life had now been altered as profoundly as a driver finding an unexpected road-block that forced him to take an unfamiliar route to an unfamiliar place with unfamiliar people using syringes instead of arrows to point the way.

Michael Jackson would not be the first person in history to cave in to his own parent's requests when the opposite of the request was his true desire, people do this every day. And sometimes, quite often, our parents (and other wise elders of the village) can be right. Therefore, I am by no means saying that we should never listen to our often learned, well-meaning parents. This book is essentially about training your sixth-sense to constantly work efficiently on your behalf for your prosperity, protection and happiness. We are talking about knowing the difference between saying,

"*No!*" for the sole sake of being difficult, to simply get out of doing some 'hard' work, and saying "*No!*" because your gut informs you that you can avoid a sequence of events that can potentially lead you to sadness or ruin, are two completely different things.

Always listen to your parents. Always follow your intuition. Sometimes the two are headed in the same direction. When you are in doubt, put your hand on your stomach and vividly picture yourself doing or saying whatever it is that is being requested of you. See it in your mind in as rich detail as you can visualize and whilst in this mode ask yourself how you feel about what you see. Are you light or heavy, is your stomach open and free or knotted and tight, are you starting to feel optimism or anxiety, pride or guilt? If what you are feeling can be termed as 'negative' then it is never too late to back out of what may seem to be the unavoidable. Even when you have become involved and the situation has gathered some momentum, monitor the progression of the situation or conversation, event or events. How are they progressing? If you have felt bad about this even before it began and you see continuing signs that your hunches are correct and if you try to change things but find the situation is way out your control, then it's time for you to take a good hard look at what lies before you. Is your motivation overshadowed by your fear? Do you have a distinct lack of enthusiastic passion for what is about to take place? Do you have any feelings of anger, guilt or depression due directly to your involvement in the event/situation/job/conversation? If you answered "Yes" to two or more of the above, then praise your subconscious for watching out for you. Follow this by politely stepping back appropriately.

Michael Jackson stated publicly that he never intended to permanently leave the *Jacksons* family band; he just did not want to do this particular tour. Below is his official press statement which vividly embodies his emotions of the time:

"We're beginning our tour tomorrow and I wanted to talk to you about something of great concern to me. We've worked a long time to make this show the best it can be. But we know a lot of kids are having trouble getting tickets. The other day I got a letter from a girl in Texas named Ladonna Jones. She'd been saving her money from odd jobs to buy a ticket, but with the current tour system, she'd have to buy four tickets and she couldn't afford that. So, I've asked

our promoter to work out a new way of distributing tickets, a way that no longer requires a $120.00 money order. There has also been a lot of talk about the promoter holding money for tickets that didn't sell. I've asked our promoter to end the mail order ticket system as soon as possible so that no one will pay money unless they get a ticket. Finally, and most importantly, there's something else I am going to announce today. I want you to know that when I first agreed to tour, I decided to donate all the money I make from our performances to charity."

*

Not listening to OPL, takes time, skill and experience; especially when it is the logic of well-meaning loved ones. Faith in your own intuition is helpful; so too is the monitoring of your own freelance emotional responses to what is being said. Internally do you feel happy or sad, relaxed or anxious, expectant or hesitant?

Base your actions on these things and not what others say you should or should not do.

11

Chapter 11: The Greatest Double Act of All Time!

Of the Ten Major Principles, there are two you should never separate

(Principle 5: Imagination)
(Principle 6: Intention)
Chapter 11:
Imagination & Intention

There was Laurel & Hardy, Bonnie & Clyde, Morecombe & Wise, Simon and Garfunkel and Lennon & McCartney. There have been double-acts since time began, but there is one double-act that all great double-acts have used since Caine and Abel.. It is THE double-act that YOU must use constantly if you are to acquire all that you want from life. You must be able to first IMAGINE what you want and then move with INTENTION to make that imagining your reality.

"*Intention's'* best friend is *'Imagination'*. For without *imagination, intention* is treading water rather than swimming; an engine without a spark-plug or like getting dressed up in your best ever outfit, hair, nails, make-up and accessories all done to perfection, sparkling from head-to-toe, going to the door... then locking yourself on the *inside* of your house, standing there like a frozen lemon. You are now looking at the bland backside of your own front door for the entire evening with only an occasional glance at the slowly ticking second hand of your wristwatch.

And *imagination* without *intention* is just... day-dreaming. But however, when you start to mix them both together... Things happen, sparks fly, lives can be changed forever, the universe rubs its hands with glee and smiles its naughtiest of smiles....

Six famous aviators had already died in pursuit of crossing the Atlantic by the time Charles Augustus Lindbergh (1902-1974) made the historic solo non-stop journey on May 20th-21st, 1927 from Roosevelt Field on Long Island USA to Le Bourget in Paris in his legendary single-seat, single engine monoplane named the *Spirit of St. Louis,* in his own words,

"It is the greatest shot of adrenaline to be doing what you have wanted to do so badly. You almost feel like you could fly without the plane."

Prior to Christopher Columbus' journey to the Americas in 1492, the only territory held by Spain (apart from Spain) was the Canary Islands. However, a most imaginative, cunning plan hatched by the Habsburgs (Spain's Royal family), enabled Spain to take full control or at least part control of sections of Africa, the Caribbean Islands and much of the Americas by the middle of the sixteenth century without spilling a drop of blood or even issuing a single threat to any government or individual! Instead of war, the Habsburgs used **love,** quite literally. Instead of military might, the Spanish Royals married off their sons and daughters to the most powerful ruling families in Europe and across the globe, thereby ensuring world-wide that anti-Spanish aggression would remain at a minimum. This had the added bonus effect of freeing up Spanish Arms and resources for use where love alone would not be enough. Consequently, this became the Spanish Empire's golden moment, where much of the world was subject in some way straight-forward *or* complicated, to this nation's domination but ultimately it was simply another case of how to rule half the world with *Imagination* and best buddy, *Intention.*

When Barack Obama won the most historic presidential election in history he did it with charm, with eloquence and with an imagination and intention that encompassed modern day technology in a way that the other nominees had not even begun to contemplate. Here are just some of the groundbreaking figures involved in his win: 13 million people on his e-mail list. More than 1 billion e-mails. There were 3 million online donors. Barack had 5 million "friends" on more than 15 social networking sites, 3 million "friends" just on *Facebook* alone. During the election he regularly attracted 8.5 million monthly visitors to *MyBarackObama.com.* where therein lies 2 million profiles with 400,000 blog posts. (35,000 volunteer groups held 200,000 offline events, and 70,000 fundraising centers raised $30 million). Obama's campaigner's screened 2,000 official YouTube videos that were watched more than 80 million times, with 135,000 subscribers. And that's not all folks; 442,000 people sent in their own Obama inspired videos to *YouTube,* 3 million people signed up for his text messaging program with each receiving 5 to 20 messages per month!

In Sir Roger Banister's case *Imagination* and *Intention* made him the master of the track (*see next chapter*) despite what his peers and even scientists had said. In the case of Charles Lindbergh, *Imagination* and *Intention* made him master of the skies despite what the dead would have said. In the case of the dynastic all conquering Habsburgs of the 15th to early 20th Century, *Imagination* and *Intention* made them masters, or at the very least, rulers of the Western world no matter what their Generals might have said or advocated. And in the case of President Barack Obama, *Imagination* and *Intention* made him the master of "*Change*" no matter what complacency or *Other People's Logic* might have said. As noted in his February 5th 2008 speech which may be worth contemplating as you proceed through the pages of this manual.

"Change will not come if we wait for some other person or some other time. We are the ones we've been waiting for. We are the change that we seek."

My point is you have your own life and your own ***Shining Destiny*** that you must follow. You will read stories of what has been done and therefore supposedly what you can and cannot do. Religious leaders will slam their fists down on sacred books and point towards the sky in condemnation of your ideas or ideas similar to yours. Scientists and doctors will say, "*That is impossible!*" and "*This has never been done!*" None will say, "*This has not been done... yet. Go for it and good luck with your efforts.*" Parents with watery eyes on bended knees will plead to you and weave your conscience to make a knitted pullover or a pair of woolly socks out of your exposed heartstrings. Everybody has the "*perfect*" idea for how you should live your life; sometimes it can be in seamless synchronisation with your own ideas, most often it is not. When your gut tells you that it is not, remind yourself that everyone will eventually benefit from your diplomatic yet firm stand. Days, weeks, months or years from now they will understand why you made your decision and you will breathe a deep sigh of relief that you did.

"You have enemies? Good. That means that you've stood up for something in your life."

-Winston Churchill (1874-1965)

As I was writing this book, over the years I found countless excuses of why I should cancel my idea of publishing it. All of my reasons were logical and made perfect 'sense.' In the end I felt tempted to leave it solely for the eyes of my son, as publisher after publisher refused to offer me a deal. This is even though many offered complimentary words and positive comments about my book.

By chance I met the son of famous radio talk-show host Anna Raeburn. I knew him for years before he mentioned in casual conversation that she was his mother. She had been one of my favourite heroes for decades! Her helpful nature, sharp wit and expansive knowledge was one of my early influences down the path of motivational guidance.

Unconditionally, she read my book and passed it on to her agent. At that point nothing much happened, but the mere fact that she liked my work gave me a fresh powerful impetus and I started to pursue publication once again. The start-stop, start-stop book process had now gone on for almost 20 years. But Anna's belief, compounded with the belief of my wife and the comments that I'd received from the many who I had personally assisted over the years made me believe that my book and my message had a chance.

When recession hit and I soon found myself jobless, in arears at the bank, with the taxman and with all my creditors. After some soul-searching, I realised I was being forced to finish the life-coach apprenticeship that I had earnestly begun. All my theoretical work and research was now being put to the 'practical' first-hand test. If I practised what I preached, could I survive, prosper, be healthy in mind, body and spirit? The answer was a resounding YES! YES! YES!

I understood that in order to assist those who I claim to care for, I must first walk-the-walk in THEIR shoes. As my wife Elena often says, *"To know your friend, you must first eat a pound of salt with him."*

I know what it's like to loose 2 jobs through sudden liquidation with no compensation. I know what it's like to shake at the sound of the telephone ring and a letter falling from your letter box. I know what it's like to have to borrow without knowing when you can pay back. I know what it's like to be psychologically tortured by bully bailiffs in the early hours of the morning. I know what it's like to temporarily feel useless. And I believe I know all this because at sometime during my twenty-year 'labour' on *The Best Possible You,* I stated my sincerity, my dedication and my committment to my (*self inflicted*) project. I stated it with my actions even more so than my words. For even when I temporarily gave up on publishing my book, I never stopped sharing what I knew and what I'd written to those in need of motivation.

Then through ***Success Magazine*** I stumbled upon ***New York Times*** best seller ***MillionaireMessenger*** author **Brendon Burchard,** whose book and video courses taught me step by step how to package my products and *myself* in a way that the traditional publishing houses were completely unable to do. I also learned about the revolutionary services of www.***FastPencil.com*** [http://www.FastPencil.com], a company I call the '21st Century publishers.' Publishers of the future, with visionaries Mike Ashley and Steve Wilson at the helm, helping to turn authors dreams into reality.

This is all cutting edge stuff. The explosion of the internet and internet based businesses is as unprecedented as it is awesome. What I'm doing and the way I'm doing it could not have been done 20 years ago! Most people are wondering what the heck they can do to get the most out of this new frontier in business strategy. I was already waiting at the station with my bags packed when the train rolled in and I think I heard someone shout, *"This is for you!"* I didn't calculate that it would happen exactly when it did but I stuck with my passion and with IMAGINATION AND INTENTION my day arrived, **as your day will arrive.** But I always made sure I remained in a constant state of READINESS just in case. I was able to do this through FAITH. FAITH I have because my INTUITION guides my way.

YOUR MOTIVATIONAL LIST

Here you will list the reasons why you will follow your heart in the attainable quest of a better more fulfilling life:

- Examples:
- This is my calling.
- I enjoy this more than anything else.
- I want my children to see me as a good role-model.
- I want to live a life with few or no regrets.
- I believe what I do/make is of higher quality than that which is on the market right now.
- I believe I can make my product cheaper than anything on the market.
- My products are different.
- I have a talent and it would be a shame not to use it.
- This is an opportunity to reap huge financial rewards for me and my family.

The above are only possible examples of the things that may motivate you; breaking through the glass ceiling, showing a rags-to riches story, proving your family or peers wrong, or picking yourself up when you had been left for 'dead' are other reasons. YOU list YOUR reasons. Take your time, add some when the inspiration comes to you.

- 1
- 2
- 3
- 4
- 5
- 6
- 7

Breathing Practice

Breathing is an art and controlled breathing is the optimum way of energising your being through the medium of breath. For most, it is a little awkward at first. As it involves breathing into your 'stomach' as opposed to your 'lungs.' Of course air will fill your lungs, but if you make sure that it is your belly going in and out instead of your chest, then you know that you are doing the exercise properly. And at least three of your first breaths during visualisation and meditation should be as deep as possible.

Imagine that you are about to start the race of your life (perhaps you are). Think of the different negative things that may have happened to you today or within the past few days. As you think of these things imagine that with every outward breath you exhale each negative situation out into the Earth's atmosphere. One breath per thought, although particularly heavy problems make take two or three quite forceful outward breaths. When you've sent those nasty mood-spoiling thoughts 'temporarily' out of your system and away from you, it's time to look up at the track ahead. With your eyes closed and mind open, look along your life's track/path to see where you want to go. Picture in your mind the things you want to achieve and see these at the side of the track almost like water stations in a professional long-distance race. Breathe in these positive images; breathe in how it feels as you get there. The feelings of joy, of love, of achievement, of satisfaction, of completion, of triumph, whatever it means to you breathe it in and as you do imagine that the inward oxygen is like a healing shimmering light that cascades beautifully like a gentle waterfall down throughout your entire being. As it does so it replenishes and heals everything it touches as it goes all the way down to the tips of your toes to the very top of your head encompassing all that's in between, not forgetting fingertips, your crutch area and all internal organs. One inward breath per body-part, for instance, feet, legs, crutch and Buttocks, hands, arms, lungs, heart, back, neck, face, head, Voila! Once you've completed that, remain still and quiet just savouring the moment. You can stay like that for as long as you like and in that case it's probably best if you do this exercise before bed at night or at a time when life has unfairly unloaded on you but you've managed somehow to sneak off to find a secluded spot where you can... breathe.

· The force that created us gave us only one thing that we can truly call our own... our minds. Our friends, our family, even our own bodies can fail us, our minds are eternal

By definition, mastery in any wished for area will come only as the result of having dealt with adverse situations up to and including 'failure' (sometimes often). Therefore **failure should not be seen as the end but a chance for a new beginning.**

· Positive thoughts have to consciously be formed with intention in the mind of the thinker.

· Negative thoughts however, will fly into the mind of the thinker without invitation, like a bluebottle-fly or bee into a house on a summer's day.

· All of your great ideas mean nothing unless you intend to make them reality.

· Do not underestimate your imagination. Use it constructively; your mind is much more powerful than you think.

· Every morning imagine a day filled with inspiration, happiness, wellness and success and then use your intention to make it happen.

· If **imagination** equals the huge fish on the end of the fishing line. Then **intention** IS the fishing line.

❊ Imagination is what you would do if you won the lottery. Intention is buying a ticket

12

Chapter 12: Movement is a Must!

(*Principle 7:* ***MOVEMENT***)

When **R**oger Bannister, was aged 25, he was an Oxford medical student who dreamt of being the first man ever to break the sub four-minute mile barrier that had hung heavily around the neck of long distance running for almost an eternity.

It was 6th May 1954, in front of thousands of eager athletics fans bursting with expectation that the valiant Bannister decided to give his all at this closely monitored race meeting at the Iffley Road track in Oxford. The weather behaved badly; very badly. 15mph cross-winds as well as frequent in-the-face gusts of up to 25mph nearly drove Sir Roger to cancel the attempt.

One of the three timekeepers at the event was the esteemed Norris McWhirter, who later went on to become the editor of the ***Guinness Book of Records***.

To get the whole situation into perspective you have to take into account that in 1954 there was some considerable doubt that a human-being could actually break this seemingly impenetrable barrier. In an interview by the American Academy of Achievement on October 27th, 2000 Sir Roger said the following:

"John Landy, my rival, ran 4:02 three or four times, and he used the phrase 'It's like a wall.' Now logically I could not understand, as a physiologist, why a human being can run a mile in four minutes and two seconds, and four minutes and one second, and why somebody else won't eventually come along, train a little better, know that there's a target to be beaten and beat it. So that was my mental approach to it... it had conspired to become a possible barrier, physical or psychological. It wasn't, in my view, physical, but it did become to some extent psychological."

And on that cold wet miserable day in Oxford in 1954, Roger Bannister glanced into the expectant crowds, surveyed the rudimentary oil and ash track and embraced his two noble pacemakers Chris Chattaway and Chris Brasher. At that moment he may have reminisced on his devastating fourth place finish in the1, 500 metres race at the Helsinki Olympics in 1952 and he may have wondered why he hadn't followed through with his thoughts for early retirement from athletics immediately after that competition. He may have recounted his early childhood in Bath and the fact that he had to run back and forth every day from the top of the hill he lived on, to the top of the hill his school was situated on. During those days in England (just like most Kenyan and Ethiopian children today), rarely were children taken to school by car and if all things happen for a reason, then his entire life prepared him for this day, this cold wet miserable day in May.

There was a temporary hush as almost 3,000 men, women and children gave their animated hearty moral thumbs-up; Sir Roger scanned the arena he found himself in and reflected unfavourably upon the adverse conditions. He then took a deep breath and uttered only one sentence; it is a sentence we could all do well to remember in times of reluctance or procrastination. As he saw the British flag flapping frantically in the wind he said to himself,

"A man in England can't wait for good weather."

The starter gun was then fired.

BANG! The first pacemaker Chris Brasher moved quickly out in front with Bannister tucked in behind. The three teammates were within record time at the half-way point (1m. 58.2seconds) after the two heart-wrenching laps put in by Brasher. Nevertheless, the pace conspired with the elements to wear down gallant Brasher's very will and Bannister signalled for Chattaway to move from third into first position. Like clockwork Chattaway did his job and tore round the track like a man possessed, this helped haul Bannister through until the final 200metres, where from nowhere Bannister found a sudden burst of energy that took him to glory and the record breaking time of 3.m.59.4 seconds.

The history books as well as film documentation show he was duly successful but even more remarkable was the fact that within the following year after Roger's achievement, many other individuals from across the globe did exactly the same! Well I shouldn't say, "*... the same*" because even though the others smashed the physical time barrier, including (John Landy) Roger was the only one to smash the mental barrier.

For it was only after hearing about Roger's achievement did the others realise that the sub four-minute mile was ***not*** impossible. Reading about it and seeing it on film absolutely obliterated their earlier well-established belief systems *(Other People's Logic)* and infused within them the faith in their own abilities that they so desperately needed to fulfil their ambitions of breaking through that wall. But Roger did not wait for someone else to inspire his own destiny. He established his brave intention first in his mind and then he did all the necessary training to physically align his reality with his dreams. Then when the time was right he built a bridge between dreams and reality and used his mind and body to cross it; imagination and intention.

Much has been written about Sir Roger's physical triumph. Not nearly enough has been written about the positive consequences in having a dream and seeing that dream through to the bitter end; being prepared to stand up and be counted for your intentions and your ideas, yet being prepared to suffer the grim humiliation of defeat. Whether you are going on stage to sing a Karaoke number in front of your friends or if you're about to audition for a stage role in a West–End musical… perhaps you are thinking of ways to explain the birds and the bees to your children or holding a conference on AIDS at an international seminar. Whether you're trying to run a happy loving household, a profitable business or another sub four-minute mile, do not be limited by the blinkered imagination of others, for *Imagina-*

tion is one of the **essential** principles of *The Best Possible You.* And where you seek to try something new and unchartered, your unbridled imagination may be the only example, the only vision where you can actually witness yourself succeed in your mind over and over, again and again before you have even risen from your comfortable armchair in reality.

Success must first begin in the mind, hence why '*imagination*' is so fundamentally crucial to *this book*. **Passionately** imagine your achieved goal and sooner or later with sufficient '*intention*' it will be yours (Only the intention is worth the mention, everything else is just gloss). Believe in it full-heartedly but also believe in it "*logically*" meaning, as long as it makes "*logical*" sense to you, then it *IS* logic. Sir Roger made his assessment of the situation and eventually arrived at what ***he*** believed to be the *logical* conclusion to his assessment. Strange as it may sound, up until then, this assessment was not *logical* to anyone else apart from him! Scientists, sports doctors, athletes and all, considered the sub-four minute mile a human impossibility. Nevertheless, all that mattered were that *his* calculations made sense to *him*. In a clinical almost mathematical manner, he felt that if he did all that was necessary within *his* equation, then *logically* the conclusion would have to be certain success... of course. According to his *matter-of-fact* method of looking at his equation, there could be absolutely no other way.

As a sports fan I have nothing but admiration for the great historical mark set down by Sir Roger. I personally spoke to him and his wife over the phone in the summer of 2007 about the prospect of doing a six-part *Best Possible You* television documentary with him as one of the leading sources of inspiration. He politely declined my invitation as he stated that so many runners have broken the barrier since then and now he is concentrated on his work in medicine which had always been the other passion that ran along side his urge to run. It was in fact his rigorous medical studies program that originally kept him out of the London Olympics of 1948! Nevertheless, nowadays he is Chairman of the Editorial Board of the *Clinical Autonomic Research* journal, the Director of the National Hospital for Nervous Diseases (London), a trustee-delegate of St. Mary's Hospital Medical School (London) and in addition to all that, he is an editor of a well-respected textbook on the clinical disorders of the nervous system called *Autonomic Failure*. Alas, it can come as no surprise that he is as focused in life as he was in his races and evidently, someone who could run as fast as he could, would of course, move on.

- Sometimes your ***Shining Destiny*** can simply land on your lap; but just in case it doesn't; **physically do** something to get yourself closer to your goal.
- Yes, do go out and buy a lottery ticket. But also physically get to work on a plan 'A' and 'B' just in case the lottery win takes it's time arriving.
- Doing something physical in the pursuit of attaining what you have imagined is the highest order of compliment that you can pay your intuition and hard working sub-conscious. This leads to the strengthening of your intuitive muscles and the galvanisation of your Faith.
- Stop complaining about your work, relationships or standard of living. First *Imagine* better for yourself. Have Faith in yourself. Make a plan to do better wherever you are RIGHT NOW(*intention*). Then **physically make the change** (*movement*).
- Instead of complaining, do something about your situation. Make yourself un-sackable, un-ditchable and get yourself fitter! Then YOU can decide the direction you'd like your life to go in. You may even find you like it as it is.
- As the great Elena Doiley likes to say, *"If you can't change your situation, then change the way you see your situation."*
- **Movement is a must.**

When I found myself heavily in debt and out of work, I looked at the faces of my son and my wife and I told them the situation would not defeat me. (My son was too young to understand so I just hugged and kissed him and he said, *"Can you let go Papa, you're hurting my nose!"*) I spoke to my bank *Santander* and showed them my plans. I wrote to the *Inland Revenue* and showed them my plans. I set up a debt management plan for all my loose ends and I got myself MOVING. ALL were willing to listen and ALL gave me the time I needed (not

without some serious hassle-I must add) BUT, because I was 'moving,' because I had workable plans, I was given time.

Movement REALLY is a MUST!

(The only people not willing to listen were the bailiffs, who were repeatedly nasty and underhand. I will not single out any one *particular* agency because I believe there is an international problem with debt-collectors who sometimes operate as a law unto themselves... THEY ARE NOT! They have authorities that they must answer to. But with their reign of psychological terror they conclude that their victims are in too much of a distraught state to maintain their balance and think clearly. Which is why their calls are intimidating and usually done in the early hours or late at night. Use the internet to find out what your rights are, log them all down with quotes, references and names DO YOUR HOMEWORK! Take a few deep breaths and armed with knowledge tell your pesky irritations to BACK OFF or you will hit them back twice as hard with your LEGAL RIGHTS! If you're in the USA check out Bill Bartmann, log onto his site and listen to his amazing story of rags to riches, riches to rags and rags to riches again. He will inspire you.

One last word on debt-collectors/bailiffs... Do not grant them access into your home, even if a *'polite one'* wishes to use your toilet, or if it's raining outside. The law tends to side with their vile actions once it has been established that you have at sometime let them in willingly.)

Your Shining Destiny

When you are faced with a daunting challenge that you feel is a hopeless task, try to somehow picture a happy outcome in your mind and keep that picture there. I call this visualisation/meditation your *Shining Destiny* because it is important that you make this picture is as bright, as clear and as flawlessly shiny as is possible and make sure it comes complete with all the positive affirmative feelings that a picture of perfection such as this would bring. In particular the feeling of UNLIMITED FREEDOM.

Now, see that same happy picture over and over, for days, weeks, months or even years if necessary. Then from this successful picture of

your future, *Time Travel* backwards and visualise all the positive landmarks of the journey that lead to your goal, as well as what you'll need to do to insure the 'logical' successful outcome of your desire, just as Sir Roger Banister did. Repeat these things over in your mind as often as you can and then when it feels right; let the image go, like a paper boat on a gently flowing river. If the thoughts conjure up positive feelings of anticipation, happiness, eagerness or joy then you know you are on the right track (so to speak). If the thoughts bring forth negative feelings or a "*knotting*" in the stomach, then you should look at the true underlying reasons why you've chosen to undertake the task in the first place as there is the strong possibility that you are doing something that is not in line with your highest interests.

*

YOU
REALLY
HAVE
NO
IDEA
WHAT
YOU
ARE
TRULY
CAPABLE
OF

13

Chapter 13: Enrol Others to Believe in You

A rich man *can* enter the kingdom of God. In fact on his way there, a camel *can* pass though the eye of a needle with the rich man sitting on top, but he can never ever do it alone.

NEVER RATION (*Principle: **8***) **PASSION**

If you've been to a West End musical or a ballet, you will see the 'chorus line' or the 'corps de ballet,' terms which denote ALL the *other* people that are NOT the *Stars/Soloists* of the show; NOT the **prima ballerina**. However, sometimes in the bland beige mix of the *not-so-specials,* can be found… something special. From time to time an individual stands out; not because he/she wants to be noticed for the sake of being noticed. They stand out because of their **passion.**

You cannot take your eyes off this person. The main action is going on centre stage but you are distracted by this performer and you can't help but look for her/him for the length of the entire show. This person does not seem to be doing anything different to the rest of the cast… Is it the smile? Is it the sparkle in the eye? Is it the high level of commitment? Is it the love of his/her art that is somehow shining through? It's all of those things rolled into one, it's PASSION. That's why we have to look and soon without even realising, we find ourselves enrolled into their cause. We want him or her to do really well.

Our eyes mirror the action of the spiritual universe. It seeks out the passionate ones and aims to place them centre stage of their hopes and desires. The universe/God/ Your Subconscious has awesome unlimited power! There are NO boundaries to restrict what it can use to assist you in your quest for success in ANYTHING, NO MATTER R HOW BIG NO MATTER HOW SMALL. All it needs is a show of PASSION so it can at least notice you and your desires. From then onwards *Readiness* is the order of the day as you are sent willing candidates for enrolment...

Tell me, what do you think when you see a group of boisterous young men loitering on street corners after school? What goes through your mind as you glance over at them from the safety of your passing car and you notice their loud brash behaviour that seems to offer no thought for other people as they take up the width and breadth of the pavement? One of them makes eye contact with you, and the cold dark stare from beneath the grey hood brings you to the conclusion that he cares even less about you, than the little you do about him.

Ryan Wells could have easily been one of the youths that you would have spotted on any urban street corner doing not a lot of good for the community. But his life took a drastic turn when he agreed to take part in the...

Trevor Phillips Experiment.

Mr. Phillips is the Labour MP who took an academically failing, black working-class student Ryan Wells and placed him in the top level upper-class Catholic boarding school, Downside (for the experiment Channel 4 is paying the £15,000 annual tuition fees).

Within a short while student Ryan was achieving straight A's in subjects that he hadn't even studied before. Top of his class in Latin and biology Ryan developed a new respect for his teachers afforded to him perhaps in part by a smaller class size than he is used to as well as the luxury of an alternative viewpoint from his new peers that no longer regarded teachers as the "enemy" even if they were still viewed as outsiders. .

Evolution has always demanded that survival went to those who managed to blend in with their environment. In the case of this particular student his previous school was filled with macho streetwise young men who felt that achieving high grades was a sign of weakness and conformity, to fit in Ryan had to be the same. Conversely, in his new school the emphasis was based upon academic achievement and less on testosterone derivatives. Although, it must be said, there is always a challenge for any new student to 'fit in' in any new school.

Whatever the outcome, if Ryan Wells continues his positive run, he will be in prime position to show the world what can happen when we award a little faith, passion and direction to our often disenfranchised youth. And should we be in the blessed position where others in any number believe in our hidden abilities, then we too can open our wings and soar with the highest. With my heart I wish him well for without faith, one can sink very low indeed.

As an observer it's plain to see that many of the strongly held beliefs that Ryan had about authority, schools, studying and life in general, could be radically changed with the right frame of mind and a positive nurturing environment. It needed just one person, Trevor Phillips, to have faith in him. And for those of us who regularly see these gangs of hooded ominous looking young men on our street corners, we have to ask ourselves the question, "What if... ?"

Undoubtedly, there are those who will look at Ryan's situation and say that he was very lucky to have someone influential in his corner, to fight his fight for him. Some may frown at my bare-faced blatant usage of celebrities in this book, probably claiming under their breaths that these people have led charmed lives with only minor hiccups along the way to slow them down because of their unending list of reliable contacts.

Dear reader, I have meticulously chosen every individual within these pages to reflect as best as I can, a cross-range of society. Nevertheless, for inspirational purposes I have purposely made an emphasis on those who have come from modest and sometimes even less than humble beginnings. Even international Royal family members featured, are here to highlight the fact that both rich and poor face daily challenges in life. No family, from any background is exempt from the effects of fear, hurt, pain, death, greed, disappointment, hatred or anger etc, etc.

The individuals within the pages of *The Best Possible You* are famous, rich or successful now. That's the point. They haven't always been. In nearly all the cases that I've put forward, there was a time when they lived lives that were no more plentiful or prosperous than most of the people reading this book. They saw opportunities and they took them, they had imagination, intention, faith, passion and movement and by having these qualities, they successfully managed to enrol others into their cause.

Ryan Wells was lucky to have had Trevor Phillips and Channel 4 in his corner for encouragement and added boosts of esteem (not to mention the fifteen-grand sponsorship cash.

Nevertheless, teenage delinquency is not a new phenomenon. Did you ever see the movies *Quadraphenia (1979)* or *Westside Story (1961)?* Let's go further back: Did you ever read *Charles Dicken's Oliver Twist (1836)* or *William Shakespeare's Romeo and Juliet (1594 or 1595)?* There's nothing new about being a young rogue in Brighton, New York, London or Verona.

In 1943, in an altogether different time and different place to Ryan Wells, a different disenfranchised 12-year old youngster, immersed in a life of petty crime featuring low level fraud and almost daily shoplifting looked as if he was travelling slowly down a depressing dead-end one-way street:

"I was antisocial... I fell in with bad people and did things I shouldn't have. I was just rebelling, I was unhappy." This youngster took a particular liking to his local Woolworth's store in Tenleytown, Washington. The shop was situated Close to Tenley Circle where Nebraska and Wisconsin Avenues met. He took liking to it because he and his petty sidekicks Charlie and Don could take full advantage of the store's near-non-existent security:

"We'd just steal the place blind. We'd steal stuff for which we had no use. We'd steal golf bags and golf clubs. I walked out of the lower level where the sporting goods were, up the stairway to the street, carrying a golf bag and golf clubs, and the clubs were stolen and so was the bag. I stole hundreds of golf balls... I don't know how we didn't get caught. We couldn't have looked inno-

cent. A teenager who's doing something wrong does not look innocent... My (school) grades were a quantification of my unhappiness, Math-C's. English-C, D, D. Everything Xs for self-reliance, industry courtesy. The less I interacted with teachers, the better it was. They actually put me ina room by myself for a while where they would kind of shove my lessons under the door like Hannibal Lecter... It was major. It was unpleasant. I was really rebelling. Some of the teachers predicted I was going to be a disastrous failure... ***But my dad never gave up on me. And my mother didn't either, actually. Neither one. It's great to have parents that believe in you."***

The above excerpts were taken from a brand new soon-to-be bestseller which is an authorised biography of the planet Earth's richest human-being, Warren Buffet. The book is called, *"The Snowball: Warren Buffet and the Business of Life"* by Alice Schroeder, published by Bloomsbury.

Parents, you are the first line of defence for your child's evaluation of self-worth and self-esteem, the whole world could be throwing rotten eggs at your child, according to *Wikipedia,* that's just over 6.943 billion (in September 2008) eggs heading towards the somewhat apprehensive expression of your sweetness and light. But if you as parents (or single parent), remind your child of his potential, of what you believe he/she is capable of, then you have given your child the strongest, broadest, shiniest, silkiest wings possible. Teach your child to have faith in himself/herself. He/she can, and most probably will fly, and fly high. Those eggs won't even touch his feet. I've already given you many examples of this. If 6.943 billion people said the sky is blue and *you* the mother *and/or* father say the sky is green, your child will believe you (eventually). It is a recognised scientific fact that a child who has a loving supportive household will do 33% better in school than children not so fortunate. Enrol yourself in your child's cause, provide **faith** and your unique form of **passion.** If passion's not your thing, don't worry, you don't even have to shout. During the spring of 1945, Buffet's father Howard, calmly gave Warren a warning:

"I know what you are capable of. *And I'm not asking you to perform 100 per cent, but you can either keep behaving this way, or you can do something in relationto your potential..."* That hit Warren where it really hurt. *"My dad was really low key, just sort of letting me know he was disappointed with me. And that just killed me probably a lot more than his telling me I couldn't do this* *or that..."* Also taken from "*The Snowball: Warren Buffet and the Business of Life" byAlice Schroeder.*

As Warren said, *"It's great to have parents that believe in you."*

In truth, it is very difficult to achieve any form of greatness completely alone, very, very difficult. I've not heard of one person in the history of time who has. So therefore do your best to enrol someone into your cause. Let someone you care about know your hopes, plans and dreams. Live dangerously, drop your guard and open up to at least one special person who you know will back you to the hilt and remain at your side until hell freezes over. It could be a parent, a friend, a child, your partner/spouse, it could be a school teacher from the past or present, dear reader it could even be your pet. For President Barack Obama, it was his wife Michelle,

"...because people understood that putting the two of them together (Michelle and Barack) *was like putting hydrogen and oxygen together to create this unbelievable life force. Everybody knew it. We understood that together they were going to be so much more than they would have been individually."*

From "*The Making of a First Lady,*" ChicagoMag.com February, 2009.

For C.J. Walker that person was her child Leila, whereas pop superstar Justin Timberlake proudly praises his mother Lynne for her unwavering support. She has been his manager, adviser, a single parent to him after she and his biological father Randy Timberlake divorced when Justin was aged three (Lynne married Paul Harless when Justin was five).

Graciously, Lynne does concede that Justin inherited his musical talents from Randy who played bass and sang harmonies in the same Tennessee band as Lynne's brother. Nevertheless, she was Justin's sole support when JT lost the *Star-Search* competition aged just eleven, consoling and encouraging him to continue the gruelling audition circuit to the bittersweet end. Her faith proved to be fortuitous, as the following year Justin landed a perfect showcase spot on *The Mickey Mouse Club.* To minimise the disruption in the young boy's life, Lynne brought Justin to Orlando, Florida, to live almost on the doorstep of where the show was filmed. And there, with the likes of Christina Aguilera, Joshua Scott, (J.C.) Chazez and the young Britney Spears, as his peers, Timberlake's career began to take its' fateful stellar shape. Still staunch in his corner, in 2002, Lynne personally delivered a petition to the White House signed by thousands of supporters informing the government of the *Justin Timberlake Foundation*, the *American Music Conference (AMC)* and their concise agenda. Justin used the AMC website to explain the message his mother had brought to the government in person.

"The main purpose of this petition drive is to show the people on Capitol Hill how important music education is to the people they're working for. The publicity that surrounded the petition has reached millions of people and gotten them talking. I think we've laid a foundation for more public activism in the future..."

As a lasting tribute to his doting mother Justin sports a glorious angel tattoo on his back which proudly displays her initials.

Stevie Wonder, whose real name is Steveland Morris Judkins Hardaway, was born prematurely on May 13th 1950 with the rare eye disease Retinopathy of Prematurity (ROP), a condition made considerably worse by a flood of oxygen pumped into his incubator by well-meaning doctors. He was the youngest son to Lula Hardaway and Calvin Judkins. Beautiful Lula was unskilled and by most accounts uneducated. She also had the grand misfortune of marrying a considerably older man (lout) who sadistically dealt her relentless physical abuse as well as forcing her into prostitution. However what she lacked in formal education she made up with in her guile. Through meticulous planning Lula managed to escape Judkins by fleeing to Detroit with her three sons. It was she who discovered Stevie's awesome potential and did all she could to allow it to take flight. It must also be said that because of his condition Lula was very protective of Stevie and felt it safer for him to be at home listening to the radio and playing with toys and musical instruments than anywhere out of *her* sight. Subsequently Stevie mastered the piano by age nine having taken it up at seven, he also taught himself harmonica and drums by ten and by the time of his signing to Motown Records aged 11 '*Little*' Stevie Wonder had also learned how to play bass guitar, all with the careful help and guidance of his mother. Amazingly she also co-wrote many of Stevie's early classics, including, *Signed Sealed Delivered I'm Yours.* In 1973, *"Innervisions"* won a Grammy for Album of the Year, but Wonder refused to accept the honour unless his mother accompanied him to the stage where he exclaimed to the audience, *"Her strength has led us to this place."* Lula Mae Hardaway died 6/6/2006 aged 76. To date Stevie Wonder has sold more than 70 million albums worldwide and is currently in talks about being a *guinea pig* for new technology that could potentially return his eyesight.

By the time you have finished reading this book you would have completely understood how awesome an ally is your subconscious, which you soon will be able to also list as a friend, although not perhaps just yet. But for now do understand that the sheer power of enrolling trusted loved one's into your positive cause, whatever that cause may be, from losing weight, to starting a business, making a speech or saving the world. There is a vibrant flame that is ignited when others share your dream with you. That's when you illuminate the hibernating souls of those around you and their beauty is seen in the light that the universe intended… from the inside out. You then you spark a sudden quickening of energy that's as if you have caused an eruption of lighthouses to spontaneously come to life; scanning the Earth in your assistance, focusing on every detail that could be of help to you, intensifying as lights cross other lights. You may have to squint, but keep your eyes open. Good experiences, bad experiences, *'chance'* meetings, *'good luck'* and *'bad luck'* and even the positive aspects of *Other People's Logic* conspire to find a way of assisting you, albeit often in somewhat cryptic ways. Nonetheless, it will feel as if miracles are poised to happen every single day.

It's important to note that I'm not even saying that this person or people have to physically do anything for you, in most cases their firm belief in you and their encouragement can be more than enough. Remember that even Jesus Christ had his disciples and literally every great person that ever lived had at least one person in the background rooting for them, cheering their every move and often giving them a gentle nudge to help keep them grounded, humble and firmly on track.

On Tuesday 1st December 2009, respected "*genius*" football coach, Arsene Wenger, who has managed Premier League club Arsenal since 1996, spoke about the mind set of his young players and their chances of progression in the Carling Cup:

*"The problem we have at the moment is people will not believe in us, and so we have to make sure that that lack of belief does not diminish **our** belief."*

*And on Wednesday 2nd December 2009, Manchester City **beat** Arsenal 3-0.*

During an interview with Oprah Winfrey, whilst discussing the movie *"Charlie Wilson's War"* legendary actor Tom Hanks spoke openly about his wife:

"That woman has loved me skinny, she has loved me fat, she's loved me bald, she's loved me hairy. That woman I know... loves... me. So I'm a lucky man. I won the lottery... My wife Rita Wilson is the greatest thing that happened to planet Earth. You go through life thinking you know the way to do things right and then you meet someone that says you don't know anything... My wife has made me the 100% man, I was only about 68% until I met my wife."

Evergreen idol Paul Newman, (who sadly passed as I wrote this) spoke about his wife Joanne Woodward in a 1968 interview with *Life* magazine, he said, *"Joanne really gave up her career for me, to stick by me to make the marriage work."* As a sincere tribute to his wife, Paul produced a film starring his beloved in which she played the central character. The movie was called *Rachel, Rachel* the screenplay was penned by Howard Stern (*Rebel Without a Cause*). In the same year Newman also spoke to *Playboy* magazine about his movie as he further illustrated the overwhelming gratitude he felt for his wife and the selfless role she played as he made his own stellar film career. His words were,

"Rachel, Rachel is probably more me than anything I have ever done... It singles out the unspectacular heroism of the sort of person you wouldn't even notice if you passed him on the street... little people who cast no shadow and leave no footprints. Maybe it can encourage the people who see it to take those little steps in life that can lead to something bigger."

Where would (ex) President Bill Clinton be without Hilary. She has been the strong steady oar to his ship, the anchor and often the engine. Her steadfast support has helped him maintain his credibility at times when his entire world could have easily have gone up in cigar smoke around him. As her career begins to mirror his (in positive ways), Bill Clinton now has the perfect opportunity to show how effective he is in championing *her* cause and how in times of challenge and adversity he will be there for her as she was for him.

David Beckham has always been a favourite of mine as his skills and dedication to the game of football/soccer are of the absolute highest order. But the truth is; although he was already great, he became the world's **most***famous* player because of his wife Victoria. She is outspoken, she is feisty, she knows what she wants and she says it like it is and if you don't like it… Come rain or shine she stands by her man. I remember years ago when a radio presenter criticised David's performance for Manchester United, out of the blue, Victoria telephoned the show and completely laid into the announcer, I almost felt sorry for him, his ears probably bled rivers after the conversation. I personally met Victoria whist deejaying at London's exclusive *50 St. James,* members club. She was a pleasure to speak with, the life and soul of the party without needing to dominate it and she had a definite liking for the older classic tunes with a touch of 'cheese' thrown in. I'm happy to say she loved my music (*I'm sure I would known it if she didn't*). It was mainly through her recommendation as well as the additional backing by actor Ross Kemp that secured my spot as DJ for Gordon Ramsay's spectacular and utterly outrageous 40thbirthday party, which was held a few hundred yards from number 10, Downing Street. Victoria Beckham simply cannot stop herself from empowering those around her, it's her passion, it's part of her character and a **great** infectious asset to those closest to her.

Why not take the time now to write down the names of the people you would happily enrol into your cause. They can be living or even dead. In fact they can be animals if you so choose! Enrol a minimum of three and to a maximum of nine. These are 'individuals' who you can share your ideas and aspirations with; who help you to feel empowered because you are sure they care and want the best for you. Individuals on the list might not be able to respond in spoken word to you but your awareness of the love they have for you is a motivational asset that adds force to your drive.

MY EMPOWERMENT LIST:

v **1)**
v **2)**
v **3)**
v **4)**
v **5)**
v **6)**
v **7)**
v **8)**
v **9)**

Today, whether by email, text, phone, letter or in person, make contact with all of the people listed above. If certain persons have already passed away, say a prayer with him/her/them in mind. What you say is up to you, but in some small (or big) way let them know you appreciate having them in your life!

Nothing that is within you is there by chance; there are no coincidences. You arrived on this planet completely ready and equipped to fulfil your dreams in every way. Not somebody else's dreams, **your** dreams. Life and *Other People's Logic* has managed to narrow the broad view of the landscape you once beheld, let us broaden it again to reflect the expansive unlimited scale of your consciousness. The stresses of the world have weighed down upon your aching shoulders. Let us remove those stresses and when your shoulders are without your unnecessary constrictions you may start once again to notice your wings; stretch them, have a good stretch, they've always been there waiting to lift you up.

For far too long have you given yourself reasons (O.P.L) not to show the brilliant colours of your magnificent feathers to the people around you or the planet at large. Your yearning to break free of the chains that you have helped to impose on yourself is mirrored in the words you 'seem' to be reading at this very moment. But are they words on a page or they the surfacing of echoes from your own soul; the friend from the inside who has had to disguise itself to look as if it came from the outside?

I have come only to remind you of your greatness, your goodness and your absolutely essential role in nature's plan, in the universe's plan or in God's plan, whichever term suits you best.

I know where Heaven is; I've had many short glimpses. Heaven is an open-air 'club' where everyone is welcomed lovingly, there is no dress code, there are no age restrictions and all who enter are immediately ushered into the VIP room, everyone. Having money will not get you in or keep you out. Entrance has only one stipulation:

You do not get in alone.

You were created in God's own image; therefore your mind was created for the purpose of creation. The human body however has been designed for a different purpose; **communication to others who believe they are only bodies and reminding them that they are much, much more.**

Whether through speaking, touching, seeing or hearing we have the profound ability to communicate with all those that share our planet with us. When you communicate *Love,* you get your free pass into the *'club,'* Heaven's wide gates open up for you and a flock of Doves are let loose into the bright blue sky. I know what you are thinking, bird-shit! That's ok, because a shared sense of humour will also gain you access. In fact the 'club's' management has put a list on the door of many positive virtues that will also get you your instant VIP pass: *Happiness, Joy, Hope, Gentleness, Understanding, Encouragement, Healing, Forgiveness, Enthusiasm, Humour, Faith, etc.* Of course there are other virtues that will get you in just so long as they come under *Love's* broad umbrella, including the occasional *Tough Love,* as meted out weekly to an incredibly cute but often naughty seven-year old boy.

Heaven is here. Heaven really is here. It's closer to you than your own skin. There is no need to wait for *'death'* of the body to reach it. The sharing of positive emotions is by far the easiest way in. Your life and all the people placed meticulously around you, insure you a guaranteed ticket so long as you do your best to *Love.* In other words; we have endless opportunities to live a life of Heaven on Earth if we understand our happiness is totally interdependent upon each other. I cannot be fully happy if you are not happy. And you cannot be fully happy if I am not happy. The Jew can never be totally happy if the Arab is not happy and vice versa. The teacher can never be fully happy unless the student is happy. The Prime Minister can never be happy unless his electorate are happy, and a parent cannot be happy unless her children are happy.

The velvet rope of Heaven begins to loosen itself when you acknowledge another's need for happiness. You are welcomed in, when in some small or large way, you help them find it. You don't even have to go hunting for someone to guide toward happiness, he/she/they are already in your life right now and the rest are making their way towards you. Some need just a word, some need just an ear, some need just a touch, and some just need a look of acknowledgement, some will be able to take it from there. Others like the individuals mentioned above will need your faith to match their passion.

"But surely," I hear you say, *"... if it were that simple, then we'd all be living a life of bliss doing nothing but playing guitar all day, twirling in patterned summer dresses and picking daisies. We all love people, we all crack jokes, we all support at least one person in some way or another and yet we are not living in Heaven."*

And you would be right, for there is one more essential requirement that is needed for you to live a life that is Heaven on Earth, and that requirement though easy to say, can be the most difficult to accomplish. It is often stated but rarely meant and the chronic lack of it within our being creates a toxic matter that never disintegrates, never fully disappears. Lack of this element automatically creates this invisible substance that is so viciously harmful that if unchecked, over a period of years can cause disfigurement, malfunction of various body parts or ultimately... it could kill you. I'm not joking, I'm deadly serious. Dear reader, the lack of this precious substance is the root cause of the knife crime on our streets, terrorism world-wide, and practically every battle in history. What I'm talking about is a phenomenon that **you must have and you must give daily** for it is more physical and more real than the house that you live in. It is number eight of the ten principles of *The Best Possible You*; it is the sword and it is the saviour, it is...

14

Chapter 14: Forgiveness, the Key to Your Peace…

(*Principle* 9): **…FORGIVENESS.**

The Key to Your Peace In the Outside World

In the days leading up to Christmas 2009, at a time when even those who are not religious may contemplate the ethos of 'Peace on Earth and Goodwill to all Men,' an eighteen-year old boy was stabbed to death because he made a "*stupid*" comment over the internet.

After spending a perfectly happy family day singing carols with his family, Tanzanian, Salum Kombo, a student at Tower Hamlets College went to meet friends at a nearby basketball court. A short time later he lay dying on the icy cold London pavement, just metres from his own front door, blood flowing without pause from his body

Resident Gary Byrne, who owns the local mini-cab office unintentionally found himself at the heart of the scene at its most critical moment.

"I went out to the shops and when I came back minutes later I saw the kid lying on the floor with a crowd of young boys standing around him. I went over and another guy was trying to stem the flow of blood. The wound was in his neck or chest. I was speaking to the ambulance crew while holding his head and trying to talk to him, trying to keep him awake. His eyes were flickering and I could see the life draining from the poor kid. There was so much blood; I've never seen anything like it in my whole life… When the ambulance pulled up, he was

still alive and they worked on him for about twenty minutes, but he died on the pavement."

An anonymous female friend was quoted by the *Evening Standard*, *"Salum was killed just because he posted a stupid comment on another lad's wall on Facebook. The boy had initially written something on his wall to which Salum responded. It just escalated from there."*

On the 21st December, a spokesperson from Scotland Yard stated, *"A sixteen year old youth has been arrested on suspicion of murder."*

A chorus of 'What ifs?' start ringing in my ear. *What if* Salum, had forgiven the original comment made by the sixteen year old? *What if* the sixteen year old had forgiven Salum's comment? *What if* either one of them or both of them had a sense of humour?

I tentatively approach the subject of **forgiveness** with a great deal of care and concern. Of all of the Ten Major Principles of *The Best Possible You,* forgiveness is by far the most difficult to communicate. This is partly because of how our world understands the 'ceremonious' act of forgiveness, which usually is not forgiving at all, but merely the verbal signing of a contract which therein states,

"I've 'forgiven' you now, in order for you to do something totally amazing for me as soon as possible. And in the meantime, at any time of my choosing, I will remind you of your mistakes in order to induce as much guilt upon you that I can to satisfy my sadistic needs. You made me suffer, but I will make you suffer ten times as much and for ten times as long, which will be quite fair really because you made me suffer first. Please do not wince or grimace or start head-butting the wall. I am the one who was forced to tolerate your behaviour, which proves of the two of us, I am the nicer person."

Whether the mistake is global, national or personal; forgiveness usually comes with a hefty instalment-only price-tag and a non-negotiable till-death-do-you-part- clause.

WHAT IF IT WAS YOU?

Firstly, I believe that you should not stick around with someone who constantly takes pleasure in personally demeaning you or stripping you of your sense of dignity and self-worth. I suggest that under those circumstances you should take on the role of being your own best friend. *Meaning*... if you wouldn't let your best friend put up with it, then don't let yourself put up with it. This applies to ANY circumstance; whether at work or in relationships.

Now, with our minds focused on forgiveness, what I'd like to say is that before deciding to withhold forgiveness from someone, ask yourself what punishment you would deserve if it was you who had made this mistake?

For instance: Can this mistake be possibly brushed aside and forgotten? Can any humour be taken from this? If it was you who had made the error, do you think you would have learned from the lesson? Are you remorseful? Are you likely to make the same error again? Do you need to be constantly threatened while the situation is being resolved? Do you need someone to remind you every day of the misdemeanour or do you think your own conscience can do that?

Unfortunately, I have to report that mental illness does exist and for a small minority, time away from society in general with the aim of psychological correction is the only option, i.e prison or a mental institution.

But then, what is mental illness?

To me, a person who is mentally ill is someone who can plan and carry-out his/her plan of pre-meditated, repeated physical or psychological attack (*outside of war*) against himself/herself, another person or group of others.

Basically, it's Imagination and Intention turned upside down and used for purposes that they should not be assigned to.

Anyone over time can become temporarily mentally ill. There are 'groups' and distractions that, if you let them, can lead your mind well away from reality and at the same time infuse your being with an adopted anger and vitriol that you never possessed before. **Learning to maintain inner peace and calm is nothing less than the beginnings of true mastery of your own life.** And it starts with not allowing the *small* insignificant things in life to bother you or change your positive happy disposition. Things like newspaper articles, celebrity gossip, the weather, your team losing a game, television, generally rude people and things you have no control over (never watch the news immediately upon waking and don't watch it just before you go to sleep, PLEASE!).

Do not encourage those around you to believe in smallness by holding them to court over every minor mistake they make. Many of the world's greatest tunnels were made by the slow daily scratching away of persistent intention through concrete. Therefore, don't underestimate the power of repeated belittling or mocking, repeated blaming or even repeated frowning! These actions at the time may seem small, just like a tiny insignificant dose of cyanide, or like a small shard of glass in every other spoonful of sugar, every other day. Over time the poisonous effects of these small doses of un-forgiveness can be devastating:

They can cower a once perfect posture, put a nervous tick on a beautiful face. It can make a young one wet her bed into adolescence. They can make a growing child forever shy, or ashamed of his race, height, looks or sexuality. They can make a girl hate boys and boys can be made to hate authority, the government or the entire world.

Satellite images, CCTV and camera-phones have enabled us to witness disturbing representations of withholding forgiveness virtually as they happen: Sacked or disgruntled employees or former employees showing up at their workplaces with shot-guns, looking for a **pound of flesh from everyone, with not an ounce of forgiveness for anyone.** In January 2005 we witnessed disturbing footage of Chechen rebels shooting crying Russian toddlers in the back, as they fled, in the Beslan school-yard, in front of television cameras and emotionally-devastated parents...

No forgiveness, not even for the suffering little children.

Our sense of reality was shattered to smithereens and we gasped open-mouthed when we saw passenger planes fly into buildings where no soldiers worked and no political decision makers resided. We saw the repeated images of American office-workers throwing themselves head-first from mile-high structures to escape another form of certain death that was certain to be more painful than your face meeting the pavement at 130 miles per hour...

The English had virtually no respite between the cessation of terrorist strikes by the IRA and the new wave of bombing horror masterminded by Al Qaeda. Reprisals for the British Army's role in Northern Ireland, which featured at that time, un-forgiveness on a new level, subjecting British citizens, political and non-political to pub bombings, market-place bombings, the slaying of Lord Mountbatten on his private yacht, the brutal bombing of the queens regiment in whilst on parade in Hyde Park, and more.

Then there was the gas attack on the tube train in Tokyo, a nail bomb on the Paris Metro; two bombs in Spain and three bombs in London. None of the injured in any of the above attacks were politicians, in fact the bombers did not wish to take into account the impassioned demonstrative campaigns by the people of Britain and Europe-wide who protested against the invasion of Iraq. Nevertheless, it was these innocent people who were blown up as they peacefully made there way to work. No forgiveness for them even though these ordinary men and women stood up against the British government and marched and pleaded passionately against War.

And as the charred stiff bodies of innocent Iraqis were being hoisted out of rubble that unfortunately happened to be in the same computer co-ordinated latitude and longitude of the approximate locality of a fleeing Saddam Hussein; I wondered... Does Global Warming really exist or has the world itself simply given up on us? Are the Tsunamis, freak floods and earthquakes the painful tears and heartbreak of a planet who was the only one to notice 'forgiveness' detach itself from the mainland and drift unnoticed slowly upwards and away, head low, unable to glance back, *afraid* to glance back at a world that has no use for Her services.

Fortunately for us, unlike humans, forgiveness has no planned schedule, no cut-off point, forgiveness will take even those who you find difficult to forgive, but need to forgive for your own self-preservation and will sort it out from there. All that is needed is a little willingness from you; a little acknowledgement that 'forgiveness' is in your vocabulary or even that a piece of it is sat somewhere in your heart... and forgiveness will take one thousand steps... for every single step you take. For the universe does not expect you to be able to fully forgive absolutely every error absolutely. Humans do not do absolutes well. You can forgive and walk away. You can forgive and kiss goodbye. You can forgive and still incarcerate, seeking if you so choose, justice in the highest courts.

Sooner or later however, for your destiny to be the best that it can be, you must let go of the negative elements and keep with you only the positive. Forgiveness's only concern is **you** and the brightness of the light that abides in you. Forgiveness asks for only a little fragment of that precious light, that is yours; that light that forgiveness lovingly gave to you before you arrived here. Forgiveness doesn't ask it for Herself, it is asked for you to pass on a small amount for the person whom you see in dire need of it. You were given enough to forgive the entire world, but what happens in the world makes it easy to forget.

Try to remember again, even if just for a moment and you have my word that this moment will be like ripples in a pond that will echo through time and space gathering momentum as it does so. Eventually returning back to you as a wave of such proportions that it might just wash away every misjudgement, every mistake and every error that you yourself have made throughout your years and every mistake made by your loved ones.

Your self-less actions will not visibly heal everyone whom you forgive. And you cannot do any more than what you believe you can and still remain honest and true to yourself and your integrity; that is fair enough. Give only what you can my dear friend; all I ask is that you please give something. You do not know your enemy and his quiet wish is that you did. In his darkest moments of despair he thinks he remembers a time when you both laughed and joked and seemed inseparable and now you are both different and he cannot understand it.

British actor Ross Kemp in his brilliant enlightening worldwide travel programs helps us to understand from almost every perspective different viewpoints of those trapped in the Israeli-Palestinian conflict. On his most recent show; a two part documentary made by Sky One, he spoke to a Palestinian named Mohammed Kadir, a man whose property was completely destroyed by an organised Israeli Military attack which claimed Palestinian lives and left many homeless. Kadir's family are now living in the rubble of what was once their home. No windows, no doors, no level floors, juxtaposed masonry hanging precariously, dangerously. Hot dessert sand blows freely in and around slanted slabs of concrete with no regard for the living.

Ross Kemp: *"How do you feel about Israeli people now?"*

Mohammed Kadir: "*I worked in Israel for 35 years. Most of us in Gaza used to work for the Israeli's. We had breakfast together, we would talk together, sleep at each other's houses, we ate together, shared everything together it's such a shame.*" Mohammed puts all of his efforts into not becoming too emotional, which proves a fruitless task as the pain is vividly etched across his face and his entire body language.

Mohammed Kadir: *"We've nothing against the Israeli people, only the government"*

In *ISRAEL,* the concluding second part of this amazing piece of impartial on-the-edge journalism, Ross interviews a Jewish man called Natan, who lives a mere 300 yards from the Gaza Strip... on the Israeli side.

One day Natan's beautiful 22 year-old daughter came home from college and as she pulled up in her car, four indiscriminate mortar bombs were in the process of being launched in her direction from the Strip. She ran to the 'safety' of her home but with a cruel twist of fate a bomb ripped through the overhanging ceiling of her front porch and landed directly on top of her, killing her in a most inhumane manner.

Ross asks Natan if he thinks most of the Palestinians are terrorists; Natan's response is emphatic and assured:

"No, I am sure not!" Natan continues, "I know people, very good people who live there and they want peace. They want to open their stores to sell clothes, or open a restaurant. Yes, I know these people and I respect them."

Ross Kemp: *"You are a man that has suffered greatly. You've lost your daughter, but you seem to be an incredibly forgiving man."*

Natan: *"The point is to stop hating and start talking. I think it all depends on people like me, common people. It's possible to solve if we start educating our children and their children to have a better life and a common (shared life) life. We **will** live together. There is no way that the Jews will leave Israel and there is no way that the Palestinians will leave Palestine. So we have to find a way"*

SUFFER LITTLE CHILDREN

In our all too recent history we have seen un-forgiving grudge-filled teenagers shoot other teenagers in schools and colleges: In Germany on 15th March 2009, seventeen year-old ex-student Tim Kretschmer went on a rampage killing 15 and wounding several others before being gunned down in a police shoot-out. September 2008 in Finland, second year culinary arts student Matti Juhani Saari calmly killed ten students before turning his gun on himself. And in November 2007 also in Finland, in the quiet town of Tousula another school attack saw nine deaths, which included the gunman. The gunman there posted an infamous *YouTube* video vowing to *'eliminate'* the *'unfit.'*

It didn't all begin with the Columbine High School massacre, which believe-it or-not is only America's fourth-deadliest school massacre. Sadly, the 1927 Bath School massacre, the 2007 Virginia Tech massacre and the Hollywood reconstructed 1966 University of Texas massacre were bloodier and even more merciless.

But Columbine is generally regarded as the benchmark of notorious university mass killings and this is where on Tuesday, 20th April 1999, senior students Dylan Klebold and Eric Harris shot dead 12 students, one teacher and injured 24 before committing suicide.

On the day of the massacre the disturbing arsenal taken by the pair for the undertaking of their crime speaks volumes about their hate filled un-forgiving minds. According to Wikipidea (the online encyclopedia), Harris took with him a 12 gauge Savage –Springfield 67H pump-action shotgun (serial no. A232432) and a Hi-Point 995 Carbine 9 mm semi-automatic rifle with thirteen 10-round magazines, and fired it 96 times. He also carried another shotgun which was fired 25 times.

Klebold had with him a 9 mm Intrasec TEC-9 semi-automatic handgun with one 52-, one 32-, and one 28-round magazine. He also carried a 12 gauge Stevens 311D double- barrelled sawn-off shotgun (serial no. A077513) Klebold's Tec 9 handgun was fired 55 times during the shooting.

The pair also made around 100 bombs varying in size and power and placed many of them all over the university; the rooftop, the car-park, cafeteria, etc. The intention of the operation was to create devastation that would rival that of the infamous Oklahoma City bombing.

The core of the killing was due to be centred at the university's popular cafeteria. Two hidden 20lbs Propane bombs had been set to go off there at 11.17am, the café's busiest break-time. Whilst in a field half a mile away, the pair had also planted a bomb set to detonate at 11.14am, this device was set as a diversion in order to keep the fire department occupied and went off according to plan, though the explosion itself was more subdued than desired by the boys.

Klebold and Harris now momentarily waited inside their separate cars in the University car-park for the café bombs to blast the café and all of it's patrons to kingdom come. Had this happened, the library directly above would have crumbled down on top of the remnants of the café, forcing the panic-stricken wounded survivors into the car park where they would have been hacked down by the waiting gun-fire of the pair.

Fortuitously, the cafeteria bombs did not go off. If that initial plan had succeeded, the death count would have been in the hundreds rather than double figures.

Klebold and Harris then equipped themselves with their arsenal of loaded weapons and marched toward the school's West Entrance steps. As they slammed their car doors shut, the first person they encountered is Brooks Brown. Brooks and Harris had a long term disliking for each other that went back years. Recently though, they managed to patch up their differences and Brooks enquired why Eric hadn't been in class that morning as he had noticed his absence. Harris replied,

"Brooks, I like you now. Get out of here. Go home." Brown shrugged his shoulders and walked away.

At precisely 11.19am they reach the West Entrance steps a prime vantage point that gives them perfect panoramic views of their surroundings. Harris then shouts, *"Go! Go!"* And they start their rampage, shooting randomly at anyone near them or in their line of vision. A teenage couple sitting together on a grassy verge having lunch were the first victims. The boy was killed instantly having received four shots at close range. The girl died later in hospital after being shot eight times. Students between the ages of 14 and 18 were shot in the back as they ran away! Students were wounded and then shot in the face at point-blank range to make sure they could not survive! Two hand held bombs are then thrown into the cafeteria. The explosions rip all the way through the lunch room injuring many. Through the mayhem, Coach Dave Saunders leads youngsters away from the cafeteria but he himself is critically shot in the chest and later dies from his wounds; the only teacher to die in the shooting.

Harris and Klebold soon purposefully make their way to the library and yell, *"Everyone with a white cap or baseball cap stand up!" "All jocks stand up! We'll get the guys in white hats!"*

The tradition of Columbine was for the University's top sportsmen to wear white baseball caps. But no one was foolish enough to stand up. The gunmen knew full well that most of the students were hiding underneath desks, under tables, behind computers, etc. Consequently, Harris shouted, *"Fine I'll start anyway!"*

Without even checking first, the pair commenced shooting underneath the desks, around corners behind shelves and counters, killing more and injuring many.

Soon the police arrive and start to evacuate the students. The movement is spotted by the pair who open fire on the police through the windows. The police duly return fire, but inside the building the events became more gruesome as Harris strides over to a table that he knew two girls were hiding under. He slapped the table twice and sarcastically said, "Peek-a-boo" before shooting a frightened girl in the head, killing her instantly.

Pupil Malakai Hall, had a profusely bleeding knee injury. His friend Patrick Ireland took advantage of a moment that the shooters were distracted and rushed to his aid. His head rose slightly above the level of a desk. The movement caught Klebold's eye, and so into the head he shot him, twice. Patrick Ireland survived those wounds as well as another to his foot.

The killers taunted the students who were most afraid or who were most in pain. Amongst them was Valeen Schnurr who was asked by Dylan Klebold if she believed in God. Val stuttered her answer, partly because she had suffered a gunshot wound and partly because she wanted to live and did not know what the answer was that Klebold wanted to hear. After saying "yes," and then "no," and looking into the killer's eyes for a reaction, she finally settled on "yes." When Klebold asked her why, she said it was what her family believed in. He mocked and teased her for a while before turning his back to her, eventually walking away to continue his killing spree.

Harris chose another table to indiscriminately shoot into, wounding a boy and a girl who crouched underneath it. The injured boy crawled out and Klebold delivered a fierce kick to his body with Harris taunting the boy for his failed escape plan. Unflinching Klebold, then opened fire on the boy, ending his life where he crawled. Harris turned and shot three more cowering girls, two were badly wounded, the third died on the spot.

Almost in the very centre of the library sat John Savage, he knew Klebold, though not very well. John was asked to identify himself and he replied by asking what the boys were doing, the response came from Klebold who said,

"Oh, just killing people." When John asked if he too was also going to be killed, Klebold paused... then told Savage to leave the library immediately, which he did, unharmed. This was at approximately 11.38am.-11.40am.

After Savage left, two more students were shot dead by the pair, with a third sustaining critical injuries; one of the dead being another to be shot in the face at point blank range.

"Maybe we should start knifing people, that might be more fun?" said Dylan Klebold, signalling perhaps a small downturn in the adrenalin rush to his insane sadism. Harris said nothing, but threw a Molotov cocktail to the far end of the library which failed to ignite.

They started to make their way out of the library when a white cap wearing sportsman named Evan Todd happened to be directly in front of them. How they enjoyed taunting Evan. Their twisted jibes culminated in a chilling question from Klebold,

"Give me one good reason why I shouldn't kill you." Todd's answer was simple,

"I don't want trouble." The duo did not let up with their scare tactics, darkly debating inches from Todd's face whether or not he should be killed. Ultimately the pair let him live, leaving the library at 11.42am.

The pair carried on wandering though the school, into the cafeteria where they managed to detonate a propane gas bomb by throwing a Molotov cocktail at it. They taunted whoever they saw but shot no one else that day. They both committed suicide at just before 12:10pm; 17 year old Dylan Klebold with shot to the side of his head and 18 year old Eric Harris with a self-administered shot through the mouth.

For a time, their early bomb-making checklists and itineraries were available for anyone to study and imitate via the internet on AOL. Their later hand-written bomb-plot showed their intent on killing as many bystanders and emergency personnel as possible and **their diaries also revealed their detailed planned hijacking of an aircraft from Denver International Airport and the crashing of it into a building in New York City! All this information was readily accessible two years before Al-Qaeda flew hijacked planes into New York's twin towers!**

It Starts Small

And it starts with being witness to the un-forgiveness of the smallest things; like grudges held over time. It picks up momentum with a world-wide culture that regularly states everything that is good or bad can be punished; small or grand-scale, mistake or intentional; if it doesn't suit you, makes you feel small or uncomfortable, if in any way it does not align with your way of thinking, then it can be punished.

We punish such insignificant things as people's fashion sense on national television and give them a 'make-over' to suit ***our*** own taste. We criticize the way other countries are governed and threaten to punish those countries by giving them a 'make-over' to suit our own tastes

The pair were punished too; Klebold and Harris were two of the un-forgiven. Well before their violent rampage, it is reported that the university had an open atmosphere of bullying by the sportsmen (jocks), who constantly aimed homophobic jibes at Harris and Klebold.

They escaped the intimidation by plunging themselves deeply into computer games, which was their passion. Here the two, in particular

Harris, truly excelled and perhaps truly lived. Their favourite games were *Doom* and *Wolfstein 3D*. Harris's gift for these games extended to the fact that he created higher levels for other participants of the game which are still available on the internet 10 years on. He also created another game entirely called, Tier, which he called, his "...life's work." That game seems to now be lost.

In any case the boys started to get into trouble in 1996-1997, when their online blogs, which included their thoughts on how to cause trouble with small explosives, gave the private address to a classmate that Eric Harris despised at the time. Brooks Brown. Brown's mother complained to the Jefferson County Sheriff's Office and investigator Michael Guerra examined the site and found that Harris had also written about his general disgust with society and an urge to murder those who irritated him.

Immediately, the pair's computer access was severely limited. American Psychiatrist Jerald Block, suggests: *"Klebold and Harris were immersed in games like Doom and their lives were most gratifying while playing in a virtual world. The anger that was being projected into the games was now unleashed into the real world. In addition, the computer restrictions opened up substantial amounts of idle time that otherwise would have gone toward their online activities. They increasingly used that time to express their anger and their antisocial tendencies likewise increased. This in turn created more restrictions. Finally, after being arrested and banned from their computers for a month, the two teens became homicidal and began documenting plans to attack the school."*

When Goth Rocker, Marilyn Manson was interviewed on music channel *VH1* he was asked what would he have said to the youngsters of Columbine. His reply was,

"I wouldn't say a single word to them. I would listen to what they have to say, and that's what no one else did."

So here at last is my point, and I apologise to the squeamish for my attention to detail during this Columbine report, there is a reason behind it all... You see, some did listen. **Truecommunication is listening and then responding to prove you have heard what has been said.....**

The earthly crimes committed by Dylan Klebold and Eric Harris are heinous and of that we are in no doubt, but dear reader did you notice anything about those they let live? Did you notice anything uniform about those fortunate individuals that the pair chose to forgive, amongst them a white cap wearing jock!?

I will give you my answer, which has so far not (to my knowledge) been highlighted by any historian or government agency:

Those that were allowed to live were those that communicated with the pair. The chosen few that were able to walk away from the killers after being face to face with them, were those that listened to what the pair had said and then responded with a direct answer proving they had heard what had been said to them. The same goes for those that spoke to the pair giving them a question that the pair (or one of them) had to answer to prove that the pair (or one of them) had heard what had been said.

Think of the personal heated arguments that you've had, especially with loved ones. I'm 100% sure that you have either heard or said at least one of the following questions or statements over the past two years:

"Did you hear a single word I said?" "Are you listening to me?" "Why does it feel as if I'm talking to a brick wall?" "We need to talk."

You may have even heard or said something as dangerous as,

"Repeat back to me what I've just said to you, so that I know you are listening" (Always guaranteed to get your weekend off to a less than smooth start).

But, why is it so important that someone else acknowledges our existence? Why is it that we cannot be content with what we know, why must others know too? Why must it be that we would in some extreme cases rather die as victims of domestic abuse or political assassination than be quiet and ignored?

It's because others responding to us is the gauge of our life-force. It's how we know we exist. It's because **true** communication and **true** acknowledgement are the two most important gifts you can give another human-being if you want him/her to feel alive, important, respected and loved. Whether it is boyfriend and girlfriend, husband and wife, school children in a playground or library, a newborn in a cot or pushchair or nation against nation, we all yearn to be heard, for we all have a story to tell.

Even long-time sworn 'enemy' Brooks Brown, escaped harm, he was the very first person they encountered as they left their cars in the car-park, before they shot the couple on the grass verge, Harris spoke to Brown, acknowledging that Harris's presence had been missed earlier that morning; and that was enough to save his life.

Therefore I put it to you that as the shooters set about the annihilation of their school, they saw the scene as not a great deal more than the video games in which they sought sanctuary. It has been said that *Tier,* the now lost game created by Harris was in fact based on the layout of Columbine University. In those games reality fell in line with the thought processes of the two boys, one of which was borderline depressive and took a host of anti-depressant drugs for his condition. And because of the regular humiliation the boys experienced in school, it's more than likely that they each learned to 'numb-out' and disassociate themselves mentally from Columbine; each day going through the motions of attendance like a sleepwalker in a familiar though unwanted dream.

The only time they could *'snap'* back into reality was when they were asked to step outside the game, even if only for a moment by someone who acknowledged them on a 'human' level and communicated with them in a manner that was alien to their computer games; in a manner that dragged their minds back to the place where their bodies stood. Not with aggression, no, for that would be just like the game. Hence the police had their gunshot fire returned immediately by the boys. Not with acts of cowering, for that too could also resemble a game. The boys would be *'snapped'* back into reality by… normality: By a small or large acknowledgement that between the lines says your role here is important, I see you and I hear you, I acknowledge your existence in this world. No frills are necessary.

For instance a mother calling a boy for dinner might sound like:

"Jonathan, your dinner is on the table. Don't let it get cold."

"But, mom, I'm on the computer, I'll be down in a second."

"It's up to you, son. But just to let you know it's macaroni-cheese, and we are all tucking in right now."

At that point the real world has peacefully and effortlessly overcome the fantasy world, even if only for one hour. Though basic and simple, the true communication between the pair has interfered with his alternate existence and he finds himself back on Earth. It's why friends and relatives are asked to talk to coma patients while the patient is unconscious. For with a loving word or a loving touch, a world of nightmares can be instantly substituted for reality, even after **years** of sleep. And 'throwing' coins at a beggar will not help him as much as talking and listening to him.

We cannot assume someone is **awake** just because he is walking around with his eyes open and doing things we have learned to associate with being awake? The fact is… most people are walking around with their eyes open doing things that should be associated with being asleep! **Acknowledgement is at the heart of true communication. Love is at the heart of acknowledgement and You are at the heart of love.**

Monaco Prison

The truest form of forgiveness encourages us not to enter into the nightmare creations of our peers and loved ones. This is done by addressing the source of the person we see in front of us and not the cruel collage they have created. Not the actions, the personality or the history of the body presented to us, but instead aim to see the universal light energy that surrounds him/her, the same light that created us all, as pure and as innocent as the day he/she was born.

By doing this you will give him/her the opportunity to escape their imagined world of hate and leave it far behind. It applies to every area where you see pain. This is not the moment to judge them on their actions, for that will only bring their attention back to their actions and your words will be your free pass into the warped vortex they have weaved.

I remember some years ago, during the endless hot (in Europe) summer of 2003, I was told by a Monegasque DJ pal of mine Herve (a true ego-less Legend), that the Jail in the virtually crime-free principality of Monaco, had at that time only one prisoner. Shaking my head in amazement, it occurred to me that there must be at least two: The jailer/warden must be also a prisoner even though he did not commit any crime. For whether it is in our personal lives or as a piece of our shared history, **you lock yourself in the prison you seek to hold others in and you permanently tie yourself to those you forever blame**.

In addition, **you** cannot and will not escape until you (metaphorically) set **him** free of your judgement and allow a higher power (be it God or the courts) to continue with <u>his</u> punishment or indeed whatever form of correction those higher powers deem appropriate to hand out. For in doing so you **free yourself** from the weighty burden of **his** incarceration, which in no way should be yours too.

The energy, the hatred and the passion that goes with assigning blame and maintaining it are like weights around your neck that keep you bound in one nervous, fidgety, chain-smoking place. For as you ever-so closely monitor the movements of the person you wish to see punished, or as you painfully scrutinise the situation that seems to have brought you this grief; then automatically you have found yourself mentally transported back to that dark place with him or it. Figuratively holding his hand to keep him in place, and breathing his/her breath because of your heartfelt closeness to the incident(s) of hurt.

You continually ask yourself what is he doing now? What is he eating? Is he happy? How can he be living so well and why is it that lighting does not strike him in half right where he stands? One testicle on the left, one the right; strike lightning, strike!

Careful What You Wish For

The act of **not** forgiving is a buy now pay later deal. It offers instantaneous, but false gratification as well as offering some kind of illusion of triumph. You are now chained for a lifetime (by a very short chain) to the incident or the person you do not forgive, how can that possibly be a triumph? You might as well have a trophy made of 'poo' to go with it (having a six-year old has customised my language).

Your continued vicious resentment of the person who did you wrong is actually alien to your system. You are not a creature of hate, you were not designed that way and the real you, who was designed only for love does all it can to bring you back to your senses as this enforced state of hate blocks your intuition as well as the natural flow of good things into your life. If maintained, this negative state creates its own gravitational pull, drawing more and more negativity to it, which manifests itself as more *'bad luck'*, more stubbed toes, accidents in the kitchen, out-of-nowhere petty arguements, more loss, more grief.

Constant hate, negativity and revenge thoughts will bring a host of **un**wanted gifts to you: Because your focus is no longer in the moment, you will have more accidents than you ever had before and you may lose money, material possessions and perhaps even status. This is because that is what you wish for the person you hold a grudge against. The universe duly acknowledges your wish as well as the passion behind it and believes because you asked so emotionally, you must desperately want it for yourself, so the universe happily delivers it straight to your front door. Also, when allowed to marinate, a powerful long-term deep seated grudge; will start to manifest itself in your body in the same manner as would a symptom of stress- related or chronic illness. A real illnesses may soon follow afterwards, like digestive problems, cancer, heart disease or a stroke.

This stage would represent the final opportunity to divert your attention from your state of un-forgiveness, to a state of self-preservation which automatically lends itself to a state of self-love. This lighter state of being creates a gravitational pull on other loving positive elements in your life that if initialised in time, will heal mind and body and re open all the positive channels that your hatred boarded up

You may ask at this juncture, *"How does one know the point in which to step aside and let the Higher Power take over?"* My answer is, *"You will know."* We go back to ***Faith*** and ***Intuition***. You may come to this realisation instantaneously, or within a few minutes, an hour a day, a week, a year, five, ten or twenty years; each situation is as different as the individuals involved in them. It is enough to say, the sooner you come to this realisation, the better it is for you, but the realisation must be real/authentic/sincere. You know when a meal is cooked, when a fruit is ripe, when a baby is hungry and when it is full. You know when it's about to rain and after the lightning strikes you know there will be thunder. Your intuition will alert you to the signs. More than that, you need not ask for.

Your judgement on the person or situation may be right or wrong. The suspect may be guilty or innocent. All the evidence for and against the accused, you will never see because you are not in all places and all minds, past, present and future all at the same time; at least not while you roam the Earth as a body. There is a source of energy of which you are profoundly connected to, which will, no doubt deliver the most exacting appropriate form of correction that the situation warrants.

Hand over all of your judgemental decisions to that source, that Light. Use the Light like an usher in a darkened cinema showing you to your seat. You do not need to see all the other taken seats, or the popcorn under the chairs. You need to see your destination and the terrain/carpet of your short journey so you do not trip or lose your footing in any way. The people around you may also see that Light and choose to look on for a while to view this amazing feature that is 'life from a new perspective'.

Who are those people around you? They are: the friend who is jealous because she has weight issues whereas you may not (at least not mentally). The acquaintance that happens to be racist, the manager that is sexist, the religious fanatic who says you will burn in hell for everything you do, and your mother-in-law... in your kitchen. All of these people and others you are thinking of right now; give them their dignity and when you speak to them do not address their scenery, thereby painting yourself into their mural. In serious times talk only to their hearts- not to their story.

Your peaceful ways will remind them there is another place. Your un-furrowed brow will suggest calm. Your non-resentful actions will suggest forgiveness as you address the lost child in front of you, his armoury set ready for battle. His trip-wires, bombs and bullets will trap you only if you allow your mind to enter his world of childish games. *"But He's not a child!"* You shout at me waving his birth certificate in the author's face.

"He's 29, 39, 49, 59, 69. He's old enough to damn-well know better!" You exclaim.

But a virgin at 40 has the same experience of a virgin at 14. Age does not give you experience. Experience gives you experience. Age does not make you grow. Age makes you older; growth makes you grow. If he does not know better then he is a child; snatching his toys away will not make him instantly grow into a man. With his own free will, a child will drop his most beloved toy at a moments notice and never even think of it again as soon as he sees a toy he finds more rewarding to play with. We have a cupboard full of ignored toys to prove it. Try at a later date to re-introduce an old 'faithful' favourite toy to your child and you may find that 'old-faithful' gets dumped rather unceremoniously in the furthest corner of the room.

Your forgiveness may not be a statement in verbal terms, such as *"I forgive you."* Your forgiveness will be the gentle acknowledgement of the pure soul in front of you that is wrapped in a Halloween costume that the wearer thinks is his protection. As the years go by, if uninterrupted he will add more and more layers to it, each layer representing a different fear. You stand before him for a reason. You are his reminder of happiness. You are his reminder that there could possibly be another way and by doing this you reawaken his mind to the possibility that he may have an opportunity to view your world. The sight of which will cause him to pause even if he does not show it, and that may be all that will be necessary for his invented world like snow on a rainy day to be gently washed away almost unnoticed.

Glen Close (to no one)

It was my birthday recently (I have one every year and may the habit long continue). I hadn't celebrated my birthday with a party in well over twenty years and since my son's birth, my wife hadn't gone for a 'proper night out at night for almost five years! So even though I was '*working*' (deejaying), I arranged for my (sharp beyond his years) nephew Ryan, to babysit as I threw caution to the wind and invited some close friends and family to the club on a night I knew was not going to be too busy. To make a real occasion of it, my mother came as well, and so did two of my sisters, Kamilah and Sandra. Middle sister Malaika lives in Liverpool and was unable to get down to London. Nevertheless the evening was going well and no one could possibly have been more proud of his family as I was that night. My wife looked like a blend of Dita Von Teese and Marylyn Monroe only prettier. My sisters and my mother looked like royalty and the atmosphere was absolutely perfect.

Then in walked Glen (not his real name). Glen was a renowned trouble-maker who loved a good argument and always had a little too much to drink. It was common knowledge he was an east-end gangster with links in extortion and heavy-handed debt-collection. I've known him for about two and a-half years. I greeted him with a hug, he punched me in the arm which numbed the surrounding senses for a few minutes-I soon got over it, it was his usual customary greeting. He asked me what was going on this evening with so many unfamiliar faces and I told him it was my birthday. I then introduced him to my family, my mother being the last along the line.

I didn't see Glen for almost 30 minutes after that. When he came back, he came straight over to me with tears in his eyes, shaking. He told me that in his entire life no one had ever introduced him to their mother! It was the first time that he had been presented to a family for the sole reason of celebration. He told me at least ten times how grateful he was and he apologised just as many times for his tears. Even his man-mountain bodyguard thanked me more than once as both Glen and he joined in with the party fun. The evening was a great success for all in attendance.

Two weeks later Glen came in again; it was early in the evening and the club was still quiet. He told me that that one moment, showed him a different world. A world completely unlike what he was used to. I replied by saying that that moment showed him the truth about who he really is, "...

which is the part I choose to see when I look at you." He said a very soft, *"Thank you,"* and walked away, yanking his underwear out of his backside as he disappeared into the incoming crowd.

Think of when you have a cold virus and then you are asked to do something that needs your utmost concentration. Or remember when you felt under the weather for days and then you reached your holiday destination and you open the balcony doors for the first time. In those moments your attention has moved away from your sickness to either the task at hand or the scene of beauty and happiness in front of you and your sickness vanishes like the steam from a just boiled kettle. It is then ***logical*** to assume that how a person feels is dependant upon the world around him. **I am suggesting dear reader... that the world around us is totally dependant upon how YOU feel.**

Do not turn your back forever upon who you consider to be your enemy; your greatest achievements you will one day find were because these 'elements' or these people were in your life.

Do what you can. That will be enough to make forgiveness turn and look at the world through inspired re-invigorated smiling eyes. Your forgiving embrace, hug, touch, word or an ear is enough to give the entire world an extra spin that will put a new kick in it's axis that has the potential to re-awaken the light in every soul on the planet. Forgiveness sits patiently, quietly confidently awaiting your sure return.

HE SEES COLOURS

He sees colours and religions,
He sees status and wealth,
He sees separate countries and immigration as well as gender and health
And so many differences that he cannot understand,
But instead of holding your hand,
He holds a gun or a bomb or words of hate.
He's vicious malicious.
He needs the world to slow down but he doesn't know how,
No one listened before but they're listening now.

All he wanted to say was notice me, listen to me, I have something to say,
The world made me like this, I wasn't born this way.
I'm no different to you, but at least someone hears your voice,
I may be richer or poorer than you but even in that I had no choice.
You are my sister or my brother though we don't look the same.
But where we came from, I remember the name. It was Heaven...
Where you made me feel so great,
And I made you feel so great.
But now because of this body that I'm wearing,
All I see in you is hate.
Let me take you back there and I'll prove that I'm right,
We can all see Heaven before this day becomes night.
Once we are back there you will see that it's true,
You are no different to me,
And I'm no different to you.

A CRY FOR HELP

His betrayal, her assault, his lies, her adultery, his abuse, her theft, his violence, her prostitution, his shouting, her screaming, his deviance, her thoughtlessness, his masochism, her sadism, his paedophilia, her obesity, his silence, her withdrawal, are all part of the universal cry for help, which always starts as a whisper. You are placed where you are because the universe knows you can answer the cry even if you yourself have not yet come to that realisation. And once again I say that a hug and a kiss and the words ***"I forgive you,"*** may <u>not</u> be the most appropriate in every given situation. Handing over someone to the police or divorcing someone might be the options that serve certain people perfectly. All **you** need do is answer one simple question... **Am I attacking this person with my actions or am I helping him?**

Answer that question honestly and you will know if it is your God or your ego that works through you.

FINGER-PAINTING IS A USELESS WASTE OF TIME

Much time is wasted by us all as we stand on our pedestals of judgement pointing an accusatory finger at the cause of all of our life's woes only to ultimately realise that in most cases we were wrong. Sometimes pitifully wrong. "It's because they are Arabs," "It's because he's black," "It's because they are white," "It's because they are North Koreans," "It's because they are straight," "It's because they are gay," "It's be... (Did I write **painting**? Sorry I meant 'pointing' finger-pointing is a useless waste of time!) And, I'm not only referring to 'crimes' such as murder, rape or abuse. I have a friend whose mother and father had an argument, the origin of which stemmed from a throwaway dispute over who held the television remote-control. Consequently, they did not speak to each other for seven whole years! At the end of the seventh year, the father collapsed from a heart-attack and died. To the very day of his death, they both were more concerned about pointing the finger at who was to blame rather than trying to resolve the situation through mutual forgiveness.

In the opening story of this chapter about the gruesome killing of Salum Kombo; I'm quite sure even that nightmare started out no doubt as some harmless lively banter even though it ended up as murder, because evidently, no one decided to let forgiveness or even a sense of humour intervene.

Fidel Castro said over and over again, *"If surviving assassination attempts were an Olympic event, I would win the gold medal."* In fact, his trusted personal bodyguard Fabian Escalante, calculated the exact amount of attempts on Castro's life by the CIA alone (*which include plots that didn't reach their last stages*) to be a staggering six hundred and thirty eight (638) times! And as he has outlived all those who tried to kill him, that amounts to 638 wastes of considerable time, resources and money.

Included in these failed plots were a fungal infected scuba-diving suit and exploding cigar. Almost slapstick comedy at it's purest. You can't help but imagine the shocked dictator with his smoking frazzled hair standing on end, with half of a mangled cigar still dangling from his lips and his face blackened by the blast. The whites of his wide open eyes glaring in bemusement as he says with his palms facing upwards,

"Those crazy Americans with their exploding cigar tricks; they sure know how to crack me up! Fabian, That makes it 452!"

In 2007, declassified CIA documents show detailed plans by then US attorney general Robert Kennedy, to use the 'expertise' of known mobsters for the purpose of a '***hit***' on Castro. Al Capone's successor in Chicago, Salvatore Giancana and his next-in-charge Santos Trafficante (who was also head of the Miami Syndicate) had been contacted by Robert Maheu of the CIA who posed as a businessman finding it difficult to work in Cuba under Fidel. The payment for the "removal" of Castro was $150.000.00 Giancana decided to try to poison Castro. They even brought in Johnny Roselli, head of the Las Vegas Syndicate for additional back up and know-how. Nevertheless, all of their convoluted plans came to nothing and the gangsters were subsequently not paid a penny.

And in another assassination attempt, the CIA gave Castro's ex girlfriend Marita Lorenz, a jar of face-cream packed with poison pills. Marita had agreed to somehow find a way of introducing the pills to his food or drink. Castro however, detected foul play immediately and casually handed Marita his own loaded pistol and suggested to her that it would be easier to end his life this way. Castro stood before her defenceless and asked her blatantly to kill him. Lorenz backed down and handed the gun back to him. Nevertheless, making the same request to a disgruntled ex-girlfriend during the *wrong time of the month* might have landed a different outcome.

Alexander Pushkin (6th June 1799-10th February 1837), was by many, considered the father of the Golden Age of Russian literature. His father Sergei was a Major in the Russian Army and his mother, exotic beauty Nadezhda, was the granddaughter of an ennobled black Ethiopian General, Prince Ibrahim Hannibal who came to Russia during the time of Tsar Peter the Great.

It goes without saying that Pushkin was ever the eternal romantic. He was exiled for six years to the Caucasus for his outspoken political beliefs where he spent all of his time creating literary masterpieces. Soon after his official pardon by the tsar, he returned home to Moscow and married Natalia Goncharova. They had a perfect life: four adorable children, wealth, status *and* universal respect and adoration, which was due to his immense talent and the time he spent in harsh exile on account of his yearning for a better life for all Russians.

At the end of January 1837 a situation developed around his wife's alleged 'flirty' behaviour with a talkative admirer of hers, which culminated in the admirer being challenged to a duel by Alexander Sergeyevich Pushkin.

In the duel, both men were shot by the other, but Pushkin died two days later from his wounds; leaving behind a loving family. And given that he hadn't even reached 40 years of age at the time of his death, perhaps he also left behind an unfinished legacy of work.

How is it that someone who believed in the power of words had ultimately succumbed to them in the worst possible way? Could not the purveyor of such intricate verbal tapestries as *Boris Godunov* and *Eugene Onegin*, not find the eloquence to wittily snuff out the finger-pointers of the Russian bourgeoisie who mocked his marriage? In particular, could he not ***verbally*** castrate Natalia's venom tongued admirer?

Am I saying that Pushkin should have *'forgiven'* the attack on his wife's honour under *any* circumstances?

The unforgiving ego of the Father of the Golden Age of Russian literature left four children fatherless. Yet at his disposal was an arsenal of powerful covert verbal weaponry that if deployed, would have rendered the enemy permanently incapacitated and his '*coquettish*' wife exalted in the highest possible way. What's left now is a timeless mystery. His wife's honour is left to billow up and down perpetually like a light summer dress caught in the contrary wind of whosoever tells the story. Never touching the ground before it's tantalisingly blown up again, the dress, constantly compromised, is never allowed to stay still.

YOU CAN BE STRONG AND STILL FORGIVE.
IT'S CALLED, NOT MAKING A FUSS.

Five British yachtsmen aboard their vessel, *The Kingdom of Bahrain* drifted *"inadvertently"* into Iranian waters on 25th November 2009. At this moment in time Iran and the western nations are in the midst of a dispute over whether or not Tehran is in the process of developing nuclear weapons, the Iranian government insists their programs are exclusively for civilian purposes. The British government has not disguised its' suspicion regarding the nuclear threat and the yachtsmen could have potentially found themselves in *deep water,* or at least in the midst of a politically staged sabre-rattling fest between both nations (elections loom). Evoking memories of 23rd March 2007 when 15 British Royal Navy personnel also found themselves by accident in Iranian waters, protesting that they were in Iraqi territory. On that occasion the 15 were paraded on Iranian television, with a chorus of western governments voicing their outrage.

This time the Iranian Revolutionary Guards issued a simple statement,

"... after investigation, it became evident that their illegal entry was a mistake... So they were freed after taking the needed written commitments."

British Foreign Secretary David Miliband added more calm to an already sober situation by adding,

"The incident had nothing to do with politics or the standoff over Tehran's nuclear program... Obviously this has been an ordeal for the young men and their families and I'm delighted it's over for them and that we can call the matter closed."

End of story. No international outrage. No expelling of diplomats... **and no finger pointing.**

Two months later and I haven't seen a single article about the yachtsmen but I have seen hundreds about the weather.

Full Circle

It was a cold end to 2009. The world famous Casino/Club where I deejayed upwards of three nights per week (apart from when I worked privately) went into a sudden liquidation that felt like a shock freefall in an out of control elevator. Major shareholder and billionaire entrepreneur Robert Earl explained all to the *Evening Standard* newspaper's city editor Chris

Blackhurst and to Piers Morgan in separate interviews. The "*Credit Crunch*" had blown the bottom out of the *'High-Roller'* market *and* in more ways than one, the *chips* were really down.

Heavily in debt, having used up all my savings to buy a house for my family, putting in all the necessary electrics and basic safety features that were needed, I had many moments of deep despair. I'd already taken a salary cut and being self-employed meant I wasn't eligible for redundancy pay even though I'd been there over four and a half years. How they did it also left me totally unprepared. I was told over the telephone, *"Don't show up for work tomorrow, the building's permanently closed!"* My savings and credit cards were all maxed out and I had no other planned income whatsoever coming in from anywhere else! In addition, my extensive research into the Columbine massacre and all those other massacres brought me to a near depressive state. I felt low. Ironically, I fully understood what I was enduring was an absolute necessity for the authenticity of my book and the people I privately counselled. If my words were to be believed, I had to walk the walk and not just talk the talk.

Doing a countdown of 5,4,3,2,1 before opening each and every bill and psyching myself up before answering any phone call, takes its toll. I understood the time had come to either go into a deeper sleep, numbing myself with high doses of government issued unemployment benefits or secured loans to help *'postpone'* my pain. Or I could use this momentum to add some much needed pace and presence to my book and practice what I've preached for so many years.

But, even with the self-calming techniques and reassurances from my wife and family; there were still moments that I did feel very, very, depressed.

And then I saw the story that made sense of the reason why I felt so intuitively compelled to focus on the Columbine feature. The discovery of the following news lifted my spirits so, so high I forgot completely that I felt anything less than great!

I felt re-invigorated, back on-track and perfectly synchronised with the Light that I'm asking you to faithfully hook-up with. Have faith in your intuition, I did, and amongst many other miraculous things, it also led me to the following article-the very next day after I completed my three-week massacre study. It's from the *Times* newspaper, Tuesday 12th January 2010, the marvellous headline was:

"Pupils' minds put to work with lessons in meditation"

15

Chapter 15:: Meditation

(Principle 10: Meditation)

Meditation is Your Key to Peace for the World Inside You

... "Pupils at a leading public school are to receive weekly 40-minute classes in meditation and stress relief in a ground-breaking addition to the school curriculum.

Schoolboys aged 14 and 15 at Tunbridge School, in Tunbridge, Kent, we given their first lesson yesterday as part of a course designed with psychologists from the universities of Oxford and Cambridge.

The project- the first to introduce meditation skills as a regular subject on the curriculum – has been designed specifically for adolescents and comes after the success of a pilot study at the school last year.

The "Mindfulness" course for year 10 pupils will last eight weeks. It is designed to develop skills in concentration and to combat anxiety, showing teen-agers the benefits of silence and helping them to identify and escape corrosive mindsets that could lead to mental health problems such as depression, eating disorders and addiction.

The course develops other exercises to help improve attention- rather than allowing the mind to be "hi-jacked" by emotional issues, regrets, worries about the past and future and other distractions. This can be done in a number of ways such as by focusing on breathing, parts of the body or movement.

Mindfulness originated in eastern meditation traditions such as Buddhism but is now an established secular discipline. A growing body of research supports wider use of the approach to address transient stress and deeper mental health problems, including recommendations from the National Institute for Health and Clinical Excellence that it can be offered on the National Health Service to patients suffering from depression.

This means so much to me, because you may or may not know that *The Best Possible You* is the fourth edition of a mutant hybrid that to date has had two different titles before this one and was originally written in novel format. Over time, following refusal after refusal, critique after critique (I actually paid professionals to criticize my work. And cried like a baby when they did!) *BPY* has eventually transformed itself to the buffed-up, hosed down, shining effort you see before you. When friends read it back then, with a slightly bemused look on their faces, they asked what my dream was. My reply was that one day all of this stuff will be taught in schools to young open-minds not yet too badly distracted by prejudice and the ways of the world.

It gives me great pride to know that England is leading the way in this gentle yet pro-active form of mind-training/mind-opening that has benefits for society in general as well as the individual. I cannot put into words how incredibly happy this personally makes me feel. All I can say is that this is one of the many things that prove there is still hope for mankind. Also, I cannot help but accredit it partly to our open-minded multi-cultural society with our many eastern influences and of course the sharp-as-nails staff of Charterhouse and Hampton Schools, the *Mindfulness Centre* at Oxford, the *Wellbeing Institute* at Cambridge and of course, Mr. Richard Burnett, the man leading the course, who is a divinity teacher and Housemaster at Tunbridge, who said to the *Times*:

"One of the things about schools is that silence is associated with power-the teacher tells the pupils to be quiet. What you need to do is convey the idea that silence is a positive activity to be savoured and enjoyed."

He went on to say that the youngsters had reported to him that they believed the course would help them overcome certain anxieties in the future, most said that it helped them sleep better and some also stated that it helped them prepare better for upcoming important cricket matches. If any of the Students at Tunbridge should read this chapter on forgiveness, they'll see that even though the importance of cricket matches cannot be denied, cricket matches might not be *the* most important thing that the course will prepare them for.

- Meditation calms not only the mind, but is proven to keep the body *almost* completely free from sickness. For the past ten years or more I've never caught more than one cold virus in one calendar year.
- Meditation really gives your intuition a massive boost in power and effectiveness.
- It also gives all of your 'other' mental faculties an awesome boost; from your reasoning and assessment skills, right through to your basic mathematic skills.
- Meditation clears your mind like nothing else.
- During periods of anxiety and stress i.e. unemployment, receiving threatening phone calls and letters from creditors, sick loved ones, etc, Meditation clears your mind for inspiration towards appropriate forms of action.
- Meditation removes aggression from your responses; keeping you calmer as a father, husband (partner) and colleague and when dealing with strangers in person or over the phone, meditation is a great pacifier.
- Your subconscious is the treasure-chest within you. It knows everything and is directly linked to the most powerful form of energy in the universe... the energy that created you. Meditation is your conscious link to your subconscious. Regular meditation will keep that link open so that you can have access to the All knowing energy at almost all times during your day.
- Meditation isn't just about sitting with eyes closed cross-legged alone and silent. Meditation can also be a walk in the park or by the sea, lake or river and TRULY appreciating the gifts that nature has laid out for you. It's about being thankful for the wonderful gifts you are blessed with, EVEN in moments of despair, anxiety and dread.
- Meditation reminds us, there is a river flowing through us that, joins each and every one of us together. Neither age, nor race, not time, or distance, not even death can separate us from the unstoppable river of love that flows through us at all times. We can be unaware of it. We can pretend it

doesn't exist. It's like putting off opening your Christmas present until summer. The gifts are yours, only YOU choose when to collect them; either some unknown time in the future or TODAY and everyday from now on.

- Try your BEST to meditate! It can be a life-saver (that's speaking from experience)! Five or more times a week is great, even for just five minutes a session! But once a week is still better than nothing. The earlier in the day the better, but to start with, just do it when you can.

YOUR FAMILY, THE SEA

Some 13.5 billion years ago there was a *Big Bang*; a star exploded or crashed and that explosion was the birth of our universe. 4.7 billion years ago, a specific splinter of that explosion became our planet Earth. Every broken cosmic fragment and sprinkling of sparkling stardust sooner or later became what we now know as life; birds, trees, fishes, air, water, humans, animals, etc. Logically speaking, this means that the whole that we once were; has been broken. The intense mass that couldn't withstand the weight of its own energy sent particles of YOU hurtling into space.

For an eternity the energy and entity that make up every molecule and atom of who ***you*** are, were profoundly attached to other molecules, atoms and energy just like yours... In fact, they were attached *so* astutely, that logically speaking they probably *were* yours. Just like there is only one sea/ocean; but for the sake of navigation and geography we have decided to call a piece of it Atlantic, Indian, Mediterranean, North Sea, South Sea, the English Channel, etc, etc. The sea is one that has the appearance of being many because we have given different sections of it names. The Human race is the same. And even if the largest part of the world's ocean suddenly rose up a thousand feet into the sky declaring its' completed state of separateness, no sooner would it have uttered its' words, would it then come crashing back down to Earth, to its' source, to merge again with what it can never be apart from.

A jigsaw puzzle isn't created by finding random pieces of cardboard and then somehow trying to find a way of matching them all up. A jigsaw is first completely whole, with no separate bits. The manufacturer then finds a way of dividing the picture into as many pieces as possible, which gives the illusion of fragmentation.

The bulging white cloud that hovers overhead, becoming heavier as it approaches a range of hills and high trees. That cloud (fragments/ explodes) turns to rain. Millions of individual raindrops cascade down separately to Earth, each starting a new life, looking at other raindrops, perhaps noticing a mutual similarity before ultimately joining again with others in a oneness of purpose; becoming a mighty river, a magnificent sea… or a puddle. Eventually though, condensation will occur and life on the ground will be over for all of those raindrops as they are absorbed upwards once again into the forming of a cloud, a cloud that has a course set for the hills and high trees.

So now, you look at your own *seemingly* separate body and subsequently you look to others in order to complete yourself. And the act of marriage, sexual intercourse and pregnancy are so satisfying because you are reminded of the bliss of being more than one occupying the same time-space as one. And although blissful indeed, that state of bliss pales in comparison to the original euphoria that you once knew and vainly struggle to recreate.

Your counterpart is you. Your mother, father, brother, sister, child and all the strangers on this planet are all fragments of who you are. This is why **forgiveness** is so important to all who wish to be the best that they can possibly be , and why it is absolutely essential for those looking for inner peace.

Consequently, you cannot attack without inadvertently attacking yourself first. You cannot condemn without subconsciously condemning yourself first. You cannot judge without accidentally judging yourself first. All these roads lead only to misery.

Yet, forgive him and you are forgiving part of yourself, learn to love her and you learn to love yourself. Accuse your spouse of being an adulterer and in the privacy of your own mind, you will mentally recall every minor carnal and massive flirtatious mistake you ever made. Judge another as prejudiced and watch as every narrow-minded thought you ever had about your neighbour's differences parade themselves like supermodels down the catwalk of your conscience. Conspire to strike another with malice aforethought and resign yourself to forever be looking over your own shoulder in constant fear of being struck in exactly the same manner, for there is none as malicious or as unforgiving as your own imagination.

No one has ever been immunised against this order of nature, nor can they ever be. Rich, poor, old, young, all colours, all races, every individual on the planet sooner or later comes to the realisation that...

What Goes Around, Comes Around.

Most of the world's population believes that the '*What*' that is coming around is punishment. Taio Cruz's 2009 chart topping single *Break Your Heart* has the line,

"And I know karma's gonna get me back for being so cold."

Taio's sentiment of dark cosmic reciprocation is a view shared by most of the intelligent inhabitants of the planet. As for most of us, our very human slip-ups and indeed our *moments of madness*/intentional red-eyed wrong-doings eventually leave us with the fear that sooner or later the essence of the negativity of our actions will swing back round to meet us like a bull-dozer's ball through our front door.

If karma does exist however, it has another name by which you know it better, that name is Love. And its' message is simple, "Love All"... Your 'brother' and 'sister' are so closely joined to you, that you hurt yourself when you intentionally chose to hurt him or her."

Karma's intended application is the spiritual blueprint of how banks work. Your deposits of good intentions, loving thoughts, positive words and deeds, your kindness and various forms of healing go into an account that multiplies in interest the more you add to it. Eventually delivering back to you multiplied versions of what you have deposited beforehand. **In addition,** ADDED TO THAT is what you have *intended* or *intend* to deposit as your planned course of your day. It works because in the beautiful naïve moment of its creation, only **Love** existed in the mind of its' depositors and all **Karma** looked forward to handing back out, was... **Love,** happiness, love, hope, joy, love, laughter and all else contained beneath Love's benevolent umbrella. The strangest thing of all is that **still is the case**.

Learning life's challenging lessons does not always look like love, but it always is. Your universe, or your God, is not as complex as It, He or She may seem to be. He/It/She loves you and He/it... (let us for expedience sake refer to this force as **God**) will do everything in His power to stop you from using your mind to bring hurt/pain/chaos to your own life. Could God do a better job? He created you in His own likeness. He created you like Himself; that means He created you as a free-willed creator; with a mind capable of moving mountains and manifesting miracles. He created you in His own image; a being of beauty with the ability to create beauty. With His own free will He created the perfect intelligent life-form to encapsulate the joyous spirit of creative freedom and grace. And so therefore to *'step in'* between you and your **free-will** would be completely contrary to why you were created in the first place. It would be contrary to who you are and who He is.

God will not step in with brimstone and lightning bolts every time there is a war, even though innocents and children may seem to *"suffer"* and/or *"die"*.**For He knows you are more than just a body.** If you threw your favourite overcoat into a furnace it would be quite upsetting, but your life would be far from over. If an arm of a well-worn jacket of yours got accidentally ripped-off by your local cleaners, could that stop you reaching out for your desires? If your playful dog chewed off a trouser leg, would that stop you making any more forward strides in life?

You are more than just a body; you are a loving source of pure energy, permanently connected to an *even more* loving source of energy. The reality of who you are is so profound, yet so simple, so majestic yet humble, so strong yet so gentle, so eternal, yet so devoted to the now of time. Who you really are completely understands the body is the perfect learning tool for where you have placed yourself in time and space. One day, and I hope that day will be soon, you will recognise the entirety of all that you are and as you look in the mirror with your eyes closed you will proudly say, *"Magnificent!"*

So dear reader, do not expect the Universe/God to incinerate ex-boyfriends. He will not remotely rewire a bigot's brain so that he suddenly wakes up without the racism, sexism and ageism that he had before he went to sleep. For what about the value in the path to learning for the bigot and all who bear witness to his mistakes? From where would we then get the benefit of personal growth, or the *Eureka!* moment of self-discovery? We would have no personality, no character, if every time we had the beginnings of an imperfect thought, God then stepped in like Will Smith and Tommy Lee Jones in *"The Men in Black"* to 'wipe' our wicked fantasies and memories clean.

Dear reader your free-will is the crowning glory of the creation that is you. Would you want to be loved by someone who had the choice of whether or not to love you? Or would you rather be loved by someone who was programmed to love you in any circumstance? Karma is love because it accelerates learning and therefore accelerates your journey to peace. Karma is not concerned with whether or not you think that it is fair or if you think it is beautiful or ugly. It does what it does for the sake of your speedy learning. And the lesson that **we are all joined/linked in ways infinitely more lasting than just through our bodies,** is one of THE MOST important lessons we will ever learn.

Yet, the strangest thing about this God that loves you so completely, is that He is not even asking you to Love Him. He knows that for many, it is difficult to love something that cannot be seen. God is not vain, so therefore He asks that you to love one another, and as you are each part of Him, you will therefore be loving Him. In this way a man living '*wild*' in the Brazilian rain-forest as well as those that are religious, as well as the atheists ALL have as much right to the Kingdom of Heaven as those who believe in God and preach his word every day.

The following meditation is called,
CLEANSING
(FOCUS ON THE UNI-BROW)

If you have small children, when I say, "*Tidy up time.*" You'll be the first to get the general gist of what we will do now. You'll need to find a quiet private place where no one will disturb you at least for a few minutes. Do this first thing in the morning before the whole world has woken upas it will most definitely enhance your day towards goodness and success. If that is not always possible then simply do it whenever you can. If you do have children, this is where Cartoon Network comes in handy or their favourite video, otherwise wait until you've put them to bed. This is certainly no time to think of professional business or financial loose ends and don't get distracted with thoughts about what you could be doing instead of giving yourself a private five or ten minutes (even though it's highly likely that you will receive inspiration to deal with certain nagging issues). Once you have "tidied" up that lot and switched off your mobile phone it is time to begin.

Sit with your back as straight is comfortable to do so. *If you do Yoga then the lotus position is fine, otherwise sit in a relaxed open way with neither arms nor legs crossed. Think about the problems of your day, or your week and as you breathe out imagine those tribulations leaving your body. One outward breath for every problem, bigger problems may require two breaths to feel convincing. When that is done imagine a bright healing positive light before you; if you believe in God, see it as part of the Holy Spirit. If you don't believe in God, then see it as positive energy generated by the "Good" essence of the universe. Feel that you are able to breathe this light into all the areas of your body as if you have hidden nostrils dotted all over yourself.*

Starting with your feet, then your legs, then your groin, your sexual organs and buttocks area, then your hands, then stomach and chest (thinking of your heart and lungs), followed by your arms, then neck and face (thinking of the muscles around your eyes and tension in your forehead), followed by your head and what you imagine is inside it. Feel your entire body being bathed and cleansed and rejuvenated by this protective, positive, filling light.

You feel stronger, more powerful, more connected to all that is good in the world. You will feel that if there are any messages, your intuition, or sixth sense, *conscious or subconscious should receive them, now is the time they come flooding in to be summoned by your conscious at the time of need. You also know that the light is like a protective force field that you can activate should you need it, but you won't need it. But if you did need it, you're supremely confident of its presence. In certain cases upon breathing in, you may feel a blockage or some king of obstruction restricting breath in a specific area. This is likely to mean that in those areas you are in need of some kind of healing, which could be via tradi-*

tional or holistic medicine. In any case some extra breaths into those areas will go a long way towards the healing process.

So now it's time to see yourself on a beach or in a park or in a field, whichever is more comfortable for you. You can feel the earth beneath your feet as well as the gentle light breeze that brushes your skin. Your mind is clear and you feel strong. Up in the distance you have started to make out the silhouettes of one, two, three or maybe more people who are coming to meet you. Your eyes are not yet accustomed to this sunshine especially as it seems to be behind those coming toward you. But soon he/she/they have arrived and quite soon you realise what they have come for.

As you look into their eyes you see the sincerity, but find it difficult to understand why they did what they did? You wonder if they feel any regret or remorse? They answer you by telling you that at the time that they did what they did they were fuelled by ego and selfishness. And at that time they managed to push aside all thoughts of future repercussions. Some might say that they thought they were protecting you and did what they did out of concern for your welfare. *Some may admit to jealousy or any of the other negative emotions. At the end all will say that their spirit has loved you throughout everything*

They beg for your forgiveness, not just because they have not since found true happiness, but also because they realise that your painful memories are a rock in your heart, which plays havoc with the circulation of your own life force and your internal organs. Your resentment of them is like a stone in your throat that stops you from taking a full gasp of air, never able to fully savour fully the breath of life. Your hatred is like a thorn in your heel, which stops you from running. You don't know what it's like to run so fast that it feels like you're flying; flying and laughing and crying with joy all at the same time.

They want your forgiveness because at last they will have peace but you, you will have so much, much more. So look them in the eye and tell them one at a time that they are forgiven. If you like you can swear at them, and even slap them to the ground if that is your wish. You can say what you have thought of their words, actions, behaviour and what impact it has had on your life before you say the words "I forgive you." If you chose to insult them/him/her then when that is done you must tell them of the good that came out of what they did to you. Tell them that their treatment of you showed you clearly how not to treat your own children. Tell them what they said made you realise that you had to look within to find love and appreciation and even though it was difficult you managed to succeed. Tell them that even in your darkest days you never gave up hope and you are stronger person for the experience that they put you through and now you have a story to tell of how anyone can succeed because you are here right now, as living proof of that fact. And in a back to front, upside down way; their actions helped to make you a better person.

By now whomsoever it is that you are conversing with may or may not be showing signs of emotion. This is the time to say, "I forgive you." You can accompany this with a hug, a kiss or a handshake, whatever you feel comfortable with. Remember you are dealing with the "spirit" of this person/people. Which is the part of their being that is pure and sinless. You are speaking to the good owner of a bad dog that broke off its' lead and bit you

For added emphasis and effect feel free to metaphorically remove a thorn from your heel, or cough out a stone from you throat or even pluck the rock from your heart and throw it into the sea or far off into the distance. In this state of meditation you can do anything. You may now wish to move on to the next person, you may be emotionally drained and so wish to save it for another day. There is no need to hurry as you will find that if you're sincere, the universe, God or whatever you worship will now meet you in your desires for closure and "release" from your past.

Do not underestimate the power of this meditation. Even with the little amount of time spent doing this, be prepared for some positive changes. Be prepared to hear from people you may not have heard of in a while and for positive things to happen "by coincidence" in the very, very near future. Also be prepared for your dreams to be more meaningful and vivid.

When you are satisfied with your accomplishments slowly count backwards from ten to one, bringing yourself steadily back to your surroundings in your bedroom, living room or wherever you are seated in your home. If you are consistently falling asleep as you attempt this stage, do not worry, simply reschedule your meditation to earlier in the day and make sure the room is not too warm or stuffy.

The main point behind this mode of meditation is to clear up as far as possible, the mental and physiological scars and debris left cluttered around in your mind that may hinder rapid progress. Obviously, for many harbouring deep grudges and emotional scars, complete amnesty for their perpetrators is not something that is going to happen with just one 'Cleansing meditation'. Therefore I recommend this meditation to be done for the next three days featuring the people you detest most in your life and then for this year do this meditation a minimum of three times in every month. This is to include new people who you may find cause to dislike as well as some of the past one's that you haven't fully "cleansed" within your system; consequently maintaining blockages around those areas.

As I said before, success is more the journey than the destination. If your desire is honourable and sincere, then Heaven and Earth will bend to meet you. This meditation will go a long way to dig up those seeds planted within your subconscious that have dominated the way you see yourself and how you see the world around you.

By repeating this meditation you are uprooting and casting aside all that you believe held you back from greater success. You will also be releasing yourself from the guilt that has been placed on you by others who may have wanted you to live a life different to what was meant for you. Repeat this meditation until you are satisfied and you would have gone a considerably long way to reclaiming the authorship of your life.

Yes, of course you are acknowledging the fact that there have been many influential sources that have played a huge part in your belief systems as well as your quality of life. And now you fully recognise what they are and where they came from. Your past may be filled with a little or a lot of regret and as there is nothing we can do to change the past, we can however change our present and our future by how we choose to view the past. Therefore it may be helpful to see it the following way:

My past was fate and every aspect of it was necessary to ensure my own unique enlightenment and growth. My past opened my eyes to my strengths and weaknesses and has made me a first hand witness to the consequences of not acknowledging my true awesome power.

My journey to this point, has given me the knowledge I need to take me to the next point alive. From this moment on, however, I add more quality, more joy, more love, more peace, more success and anything else I desire to make my onward journey not just about how to stay alive or simply how to get by, but a new rewarding journey of self-discovery, personal achievement and unrestrained joy.

My onward path is now about truly living the life of my dreams and waking up excited each and every day with the full understanding that I have the most authorative say in my own shining destiny.

During this or any other meditation, you may get a slight-heavy feeling of pressure between the eyes just above the bridge of the nose. If you have a '*unibrow*'(one continuous eyebrow), then I'm referring to dead centre of that.

Don't worry about this feeling of 'pressure' at that point, it is not a distraction; in fact it is a statement of your high quality focus and concentration during the session. Always aim to get that 'sensation' and if you have a '*uni-brow*' please tidy that up!

The Three Minute Quickie

Don't pretend you don't enjoy a quickie from time to time! For optimum results, meditating first thing in the morning before fully getting out of bed and last thing before going to sleep is THE ideal. Unfortunately, this scenario isn't always practical when dealing with family life, work commitments and all the unexpected trials 24 hours can throw at you. So instead of these twice-daily concentrated meditations, when you are short on time, say a quick but sincere prayer asking for guidance in all that you say, do, hear and see. This should take no more than two-three minutes.

Ask to see and experience 'good' and 'beautiful'things this day. And before you go to sleep at night, if you're way too tired to meditate, then say a sincere three-minute prayer of thanks for the goodness and 'beauty' that you witnessed during your awake time and be 'grateful' for your blessings, for you have many. You don't even have to say your prayer out aloud (but please picture in your mind the blessings that you are being grateful for). You will soon find, the more you notice them, the more they will increase! And don't watch sad or depressing News shows before going to bed! Instead, watch a comedy or something with an uplifting message. This is because your mood first thing in the morning is largely dependant on your predominating thoughts last thing at night. And likewise, a negative News reports at the **start** of your day can put you in a negative state for the rest of the day. A meditation or a three-minute quickie prayer of gratitude can really set you up so that the days muddy murky waters wash over you without staining you, your thoughts or your actions. Never forget to meditate properly when you have the chance, but yes, we do love a quickie!

(Being in a picturesque place, or beholding a beautiful view, scene or even picture can be like a sudden 'shot' of meditation to the soul. Also, listening to to certain types of music and being in positive loving company can create a calming of the senses akin to meditation. Lastly, the act of making love, with someone you LOVE, that loves you back; will also create a similar bliss.)

ALL YOU NEED is...

So, here is the listed

10 Principles of The Best Possible You

They are:

1. Open-Mindedness
2. Intuition
3. Faith
4. Readiness
5. Imagination
6. Intention
7. Movement
8. Passion
9. Forgiveness
10. Meditation

I've sort of 'hidden' the list at the back of this chapter because I wanted it to be like a 'gift' to those who took the time to read this far, hopefully 'digesting' fully the stories/examples that I wrote below the 'principles.' Essentially the 10 are just words. But infused together they represent the most potent mix of forces in the universe. And I say that without wincing.

For it is possible to utilise any 9 of the above principles and be very successful (in fact you could use much less than 9), but add the one that you missed from the list, whichever one you chose to leave out and upon its' inclusion you will find 'great peace' along with the 'great success' or 'great success' along with the 'great peace.' And the term 'great' applies to your sense of the word, not anybody else's.

Of course it may seem that I have left out many virtuous profound words which could easily fit in here; words such as: Confidence, Trust, and the most obvious omittion, 'Self-belief.' But with the sincere application of the above 10, everything that needs to be included will be.

For example if you have 'Faith,' then 'Confidence' will be an automatic by-product. If you use your 'Intuition,' you will know who you should 'Trust' and how far he/she should be trusted. And 'Self-belief' will come when you start to see results and your 'Imagination' has been stretched enough to include the idea of your imminent success.

16

Chapter 16: The Key to a Long Life... and Rest-Filled Nights

BEING POLITE USUALLY MEANS ALLOWING OTHERS BEFORE YOURSELF. BUT WITH FORGIVING, IF YOU CAN'T FORGIVE YOURSELF FIRST, YOU'LL NEVER BE ABLE TO FORGIVE OTHERS.

Chapter 16
SELF-FORGIVENESS

Most people will vaguely remember the approximate date of the invasion of Kuwait by Saddam Hussein and the Iraqi Republican Guard. I will, but for a different reason to most individuals. The Saturday night before that historic event I was deejaying in a famous London club called Tokyo Joe when it was invaded by a lone terrorist armed with a rifle, a pistol and an explosive booby-trapped package strapped to his body with a red detonator switch in his left palm (once you've been in that situation, you never forget the colour of a detonator switch, trust me). This true story was covered by world media, but was overlooked because literally six hours later Saddam's forces entered Kuwait.

The terrorists' intention was to take esteemed members of various Middle-Eastern Royal families hostage and to somehow exchange them for his comrades held in international prisons.

He blasted chunks out of the clubs masonry, ordered everyone into groups of nationalities and then proceeded to tell us what he was going to do to all those who did not co-operate with his every wish. It didn't sound pretty.

At first we were uncomfortably crouched down in silence for more than two hours. During that time I prayed; continually asking God for guidance, to somehow lead me through this most surreal of circumstances. Then everyone jumped as the fire alarm went off! The terrorist suddenly became even more nervous and agitated, waving his rifle around like a man possessed, shouting that he would blow us all up with just one press of the detonator switch if he found out that anyone was responsible for purposely setting off the alarms activation.

Using profane language he asked if anyone knew how to switch the alarm off. Fortunately for all the other members of staff, their workstations were right next to emergency exits and so when the gunman entered the club, those positioned by the toilets, bars, coatroom, front desk etc, were able to make speedy getaways. As the DJ, I was not so well positioned. For all intents and purposes, I was the sole remaining member of staff, the only one left who knew how to turn off the blaring alarm.

"You DJ, you know where the alarm is?" He said pointing his rifle at me. The fact that I still had my headphones around my neck must have been the prime give-away to my vocational status. I answered in the affirmative.

"Well go and switch it off then! Or would you rather I go crazy down here with all your customers?"

I got up and walked to the alarm, which was situated back upstairs close to the door of the main entrance and as I reached up to pull down the lever, a hand gabbed my wrist and another went around my mouth, a quiet but commanding voice then said,

"We'll take care of that."

In less than a second I found myself on the outside of the club staring at four masked SAS men and a police chief. Guns were pointed in my direction; all traffic had been diverted and in it's place were rows of blacked out Special Units vans, I couldn't tell you if they belonged to the Police or the Army, in any case they were extremely high tech as I soon found out when I was led inside one.

The siege of Tokyo Joe was over in twelve hours. Whether he knew it or not, the barman put huge quantities of alcohol in every drink the gunman asked for and by all accounts, he downed quite a few. Every time he turned round to fill up, two more people would leg-it out the back exit. By eleven thirty in the morning the remaining wily, hostages managed to convince him that if he put down his weapons and un-strapped his explosives belt, then they would allow him to mingle with them as they all made their way out into the morning sunshine.

Feeling depressed and miserable and having knelt down in his own broken glass, our would-be hostage taker was just about ready for some new ideas and after some consideration, he finally agreed.

Placing his pistol on the inside of his jacket, he removed all the other weapons and marched upstairs within the centre of the group of hostages, merging in perfectly. The only thing is that everyone who managed to escape earlier gave the police greater detail to the description they had of the suspect. And when he exited the club and found an assortment of handguns and rifles pointed at him he was the only one to throw his hands up while everybody else dived for cover.

As comical as it all may have turned out, the whole event could have had horrific consequences. No one was killed or even hurt, apart from the hostage taker who bloodied his knee.

From that moment on my life looked different. Coming so close to death gave me an instantly fresh outlook on life. I started to notice the amount of superficiality I had around me and I began to sort the wheat from the chaff. I travelled a lot more and I was much more open to new ideas and new influences. I no longer felt the need to wait for the 'appropriate moment' to give obvious signs of love and/or appreciation to those around me who needed or deserved it. And I became much more spontaneous and intuitive. The whole experience I believe was the second most important catalyst that opened my modest but clear intuitive abilities and lifted my perception and perspectives on life. I went to work on that Saturday night as one person and by Monday morning I was someone almost completely different, even though (perhaps unfortunately, as most would say) my looks had not changed.

What does this story have to do with forgiveness? Well, one other un-welcomed 'gift' of the Tokyo Joe siege was an excruciating migraine that lasted three months, which was due (I've been since told by psychologists) to my feelings of guilt for having been one of the first to leave the scene while people I knew were still captive.

Learning to forgive yourself is as important as forgiving others for unless you can forgive yourself, you will find it impossible to forgive anybody else.

According to doctors, 40% of men who die whilst having an affair; actually die whilst in the act of having sex with their mistress. This rather inconvenient phenomenon is not necessarily because the mistresses are so dangerously good at the art of making love, it's simply because although the adulterer is enjoying himself, he is also suppressing an intense amount of guilt. This un-forgiveness of his own actions reaches its (can I say) climactic peak for obvious reasons during the sex act. Not knowing if you're coming or going can be tricky!

TWO DEATH PENALTIES

I'm not loyal to any particular newspaper. Usually, I tend to glance through them all and then choose the one that has the most interesting or most uplifting stories for the day. On Tuesday 24th march 2009, I was in my local corner-shop doing my usual thumbing through the tabloids and broadsheets when a curious story caught my eye in the ***Independent.*** It involved stroke victim, James Brewster, who, lying on his deathbed and driven by guilt, felt compelled to finally confess to a murder he committed in Tennessee, way back in 1977.

Brewster had shot his neighbour Jimmy Carroll, in a jealous rage because he believed he was trying to seduce his wife, Dorothy. After the original arrest, Brewster Jumped bail and fled to Oklahoma to start a new life in with his wife under the assumed names of Michael and Dorothy Anderson.

Thirty-two years later, a dying 58 year-old Brewster realised in his final breathless moments that he *"Wanted to cleanse his soul"* in order to meet his 'maker' with a clear conscience. So he did the only honourable thing a dying man could do, he called the police back in Tennessee and confessed his crime.

Then the strangest thing happened, the symptoms of his *'fatal'* illness miraculously evaporated and within days he was completely healed! Nevertheless, Brewster voluntarily surrendered himself to the authorities in Hohenwald, where he may ultimately face the death penalty.

- ❊ Not forgiving yourself can lead to severe health problems, even 'death' itself can be a symptom of lack of self-forgiveness.
- ❊ One of the quickest ways to self-forgive; is to 'confess.' Either to authorities, your religious leader or whoever it is that you feel you have wronged
- ❊ It is more difficult to forgive others if you find it difficult to forgive yourself.
- ❊ The best way to avoid guilt feelings is to understand when your intuition is trying to tell you that you are about to make a mistake... **ALWAYS listen to your intuition!** This way you will avoid situations where you'll need to forgive yourself.
- ❊ You may not have to forgive yourself too often if you learn quickly that embarrassment and Pride are like two mean cannibals that aim to keep you marinated in guilt for as long as possible before they eat you up for good... If you intuitively feel you should warn someone, help someone, hug someone, advise someone, be truthful with someone-even though it will hurt them AND you... DO IT! You may never be able to forgive yourself if anything untoward occurred after you had the chance to be the saviour of a friend (or stranger).
- ❊ Self-forgiveness isn't a way of overlooking your own mistakes so that you can commit the same mistakes as often as you like without fear of guilt. Self-forgiveness is about owning your mistake in a way that let's others know that not only have you learned from it but you can also teach the value of your lesson. This creation of 'positive' energy from what started

out as 'negative' energy helps the mind, body and spirit to flourish in a healthy way, rather than causing sickness.

17

Chapter 17: The 'Lighter' Side of Death

It's quite a challenge to write about something that does not exist, at least not in the literal sense of the word. Do other caterpillars think their comrades are 'dead' when they see them encased in the chrysalis, a 'living' box that looks remarkably like a coffin? Would a caterpillar even recognise a butterfly?

CHANGE IS NOT DEATH.

More than twenty years ago I had an out-of-body experience, otherwise called a Near-Death- Experience, the profound nature of it compelled me to find out more about the phenomenon. I attended lectures, seminars and workshops; I read books and listened to anyone who had been through anything remotely similar to what I had experienced. A long time friend of mine, Ron Smothermon, author of the ***Man Woman*** books, told me how one day he arrived home early to find a burglar ransacking his house. When he confronted the thief, he was repeatedly stabbed by him over and over again and part-way into the frenzy Ron noticed a bright white light behind his attacker. The light seemed to be slowly expanding from the far corner of the room.

The attacker (who was high on drugs) raised his hand above his head, presumably with the intent of sticking the knife into Rons' neck… but then according to Ron, everything stopped. The pain stopped. The vicious attack stopped. Time literally stood still. The only thing that shifted was the size of the light, which had started off looking like a pocket flashlight in the corner of the hallway, to what was now a hall that was completely engulfed in a brilliant clear sparkling light. So bright that the staircase and back walls were faded out of sight. Then there came a voice to Ron, *"Will you come now or later?"* Ron's only thought was of his son… and in a flash the brilliant light doubled back in on itself, vanished completely and the frenzy was resumed. The attacker's knife came down, not into Ron's neck, but instead the knife BROKE on Ron's collarbone. The assailant then exited the house in a wild panic, but was caught by police soon after.

During a three-day seminar in which the main topic was the *Near-Death-Experience;* a woman spoke of how whilst going at high speed down the motorway she hit the central reservation and her car pitched up as it somersaulted in mid-air. Half-way through the flip, while off the ground, the car stopped spinning. With her car suspended in the air and everything around her completely motionless, the woman undid her seat belt, climbed out of the window onto the side of her car (as it was tilted up at a 45 degree angle) five-feet off the ground. She claimed she heard a similar question, *" Are you now ready or will you come later?"* And upon thinking about how 'needed' she was in her work and family life she replied, "Later". She then got back into her car, buckled her seat belt and wound the window back up. The fright-fest continued. Her car flipped and bounced diagonally across three lanes of oncoming traffic… Many broken bones, but she lived to tell the tale.

These accounts and many more similar stories are far from rare. How I came to seek out these people and their experiences was mainly due to my own experience that has remained imprinted on my consciousness as if it were branded there by a red-hot poker this morning!

When I was twenty–two, I was worked in a famous London department store in Knightsbridge (not that one, the other one) during the day, whilst deejaying for just one warm up session at a West End club once a week. I also did any other mobile DJ jobs my schedule could handle.

At that time I didn't have a car so I would often walk home to Clapham South after usually getting the night bus to either Lavender Hill or Clapham Common. Without a car I couldn't help but work up an appetite with all of the lifting, walking and getting on and off buses with my heavy record cases.

When I arrived home I would inevitably have my usual bowl of cornflakes and a marmalade sandwich before I got into bed. I would take a bite of my sandwich and a spoonful of cornflakes and swallow them down at the same time. Not only did it save time but I also enjoyed the tangy mix. Not long after, I would be tucked up in bed fast asleep. But this particular night I didn't sleep very well.

I felt very uncomfortable and quickly understood that I had consumed too much, too quickly and lay down too fast without having let my food digest properly. So I got out of bed and decided to make myself a cup of tea but was overcome by the strangest of sensations… I was light-headed and for some insane reason my feet did not want to remain on the ground. I looked over my shoulder and saw a sight that I'll never forget… My own body motionless on the bed!

I held on to my chest of drawers and tried to work out the situation and for a moment I just stood there catatonic, looking at myself on the bed. The door was slightly ajar and the family cat walked in and got comfortable at the base of my bed where the sheets crumpled at the floor. As I tried to come to terms with the urge my feet had to rise up off the floor, I held on to the chest of drawers to keep myself grounded. I scanned the room to see if anything was different as of course I thought this must be a dream. I noticed that there was a small, tiny hole in the ceiling that I had never seen before and what's more that hole seemed to be getting larger with every passing moment.

Like a hammer to my chest, I came to the stark conclusion that I was dead. But I also realised that I would be disappointing a lot of people with my 'thoughtless timing'. So in order to offer up some sort of apology I thought the least I could do would be to write a note to those who were expecting me to either meet with them or do something for them.

So I went round my room hunting for a pen and paper holding on to the mantle-piece, my sofa, the coffee table, all just to make sure that I didn't float up too far off the ground and end up on the ceiling. When I looked up again I could see that the widening hole had now become large enough for me to float clean through without touching the sides and I could clearly see the star filled sky above.

This night, the stars were different; they sparkled brighter than I'd ever seen them shine and they looked somehow close enough to touch. And from beyond the stars there seemed to emanate a kind of music, the likes of which I had never heard before nor since; unfamiliar to my ears yet completely familiar to my soul. It was as if up there was a party or gathering and I was the guest of honour. At that moment, it felt like the most natural thing on earth to do was just to let go and float and float and float... But first I HAD to do my list. I wanted to do the list /notes/apologies to all those that I knew I was leaving behind, especially as I had made verbal and non-verbal agreements with so many people. But oh the music, the music was so unbelievably beautiful and melodic, calming and soul soothing. I couldn't recognise any particular musical instrument, but they felt like the most beautiful melodies that I would ever hear... But, shaking my distracted head; still, I HAD to get back to my list, *"Heaven help me do this list!"* I thought.

Finally I found pen and paper and I managed to wedge one foot underneath a chair, the other under the coffee table and like a weightless astronaut I began to write at random, my 'apology' notes to those it concerned.

First my little sister was expecting me to take her to the Girl-Guides that day and to meet her afterward as well. Second, I promised my friend Colette that I would arrange a job interview for her at the place that I worked; she was really looking forward to it. Third, I had borrowed some money from my mother to buy some mobile disco equipment and I hadn't even started to pay her back, which felt a little inconsiderate and I didn't feel at all comfortable with that; and so the list went on. I went through two sheets of A4 and realised that I needed more paper. I also understood that as attractive is it was; the invitation for me to ascend up to that heavenly place was an invitation that I could not possibly accept at this particular time. It went way beyond inconvenient; it was completely unfair to everyone that knew me and it threw their plans as well as my own completely out of the window or ceiling. Just in case you are wondering, I don't do drugs and laugh if you like, but I only 'drink' on special occasions or a *little* brandy if I have a sore throat.

I looked up at the ceiling and the open space started to close. The glittering stars and the sound of all the beautiful songs began to grow evermore faint. I realised that even in my very normal hum-drum life, I had simple duties to fulfil that I could not leave to anyone else to do. I made my choice to stay. The ceiling closed completely and I stepped back into my body and within moments I threw up my snack all over my bed.

Dizzy, I ran into the bathroom and cleaned myself up, washed my hair four times and put my shirt in the dustbin. I then tried to make some sense out of what had happened to me that night. Was it a dream or was it an extension of reality that I simply unfamiliar with... **The list!**I ran back into the bedroom and looked all over for the pages of apologies that I vividly recalled writing, but I couldn't find a thing. Yes, the pen and the paper were in the room but they were both still inside a drawer and had not been touched. So then maybe it was a dream, I leaned up against the chest of drawers and I looked back at the bed... Still asleep was my cat, who I remember walked in partway through my incredible experience. I knelt down and stroked it.

Dear friend, you do not have to die to get to Heaven. Heaven is in the smile of your child, your partner's hand on your face, Springs urgency and Autumn's amazing colours. Heaven is in EVERYONE you LOVE and EVERYTHING you LOVE. Heaven is HERE AND NOW, you may see it even better if you close your eyes.

Earth is like a beautiful waiting room, a bus station or at worst a tough boot camp where we get the chance to see how well we've learned the repeated lessons that have been presented to us. Our bodies, though a little cumbersome at times, are particularly well suited to the lessons of **consequence of thought and actions.** You are not here for very long, but as you pass through, it makes sense to unpack and use the vast array of gifts that your eternal spirit brought with you: your creativity, your personality, your compassion, your talents and your intuition, etc.

We cannot all be visionaries, we won't all be geniuses, we were not ALL supposed to be. I can be the best possible me and you can be the best possible you. When the time is right and when you and what made you are ready, you will be welcomed onto the beaches of Heaven by friends, family and adoring fans alike. But be certain, be 100% certain, **it's not dying that takes you to Heaven, it's living**... Living a life that's full. Living a life where you show your skills, passions, talents and character. A life of successes and mistakes but few regrets. And a life of keeping your promises, to your friends, family and ... most of all, to your potential.

It goes without saying that I cannot possibly know why every individual '*dies,*' but I do know what keeps us alive. And I know that we often take these things for granted.

So before we come to this books end, I need to ask one last favour of you. Three small 'Promise' lists:

List number (1) would feature a list of five things that you have promised to do, which will start soon, or have already started. They may last a lifetime but they are ongoing as of now, or within the next couple of weeks. Things like taking the kids to school, getting fit, baking a show-stopping cake or amazing meal, doing something that has been requested by a friend or family member that will be personalised by <u>your</u> unique touch.

LIST ONE: (SHORT/NOW)

1.

2.

3.

4.

5.

List number (2) is list is of the things that you have promised to do mid-term, ie, like changing your job, finish studying, take the kids on holiday, teach a friend or child a skill like reading, swimming or baking, etc. It's **very** important that you write the dates for the commencement of the items on your number 2 list and that you stick to them. Do not make excuses, just get your funky groove on.

LIST. TWO (MID-IMMINENT)

1.

2.

3.
4
5.

List number (3) is a list of things that you have promised yourself for the long-term, like starting a family, or a business, or writing a book, learning a new language, mentoring, volunteering or doing some kind of study course. Becoming financially independent. It's important that you also put a date to these long term goals too, and hold yourself to your own agreement.

Before you arrived on this Earthly plane you made a promise to yourself, to live to your potential. We were not all destined to be visionaries, trail-blazers, saints or presidents; the only promise you made back then was to be the best possible you! No more, but certainly, no less. To your own eyes, it sometimes looks as if you were cast out into the choppy wind-lashed sea without even a lifeboat to help you back to shore. To your eyes yes, that's how it seems. That you requested your own course as well as all the people that you have met along the way seems quite absurd, especially as you never saw yourself as a sado-masochist. That you asked for this level of learning to enable you to teach those closest to you by just living your life seems WAY TOO well planned for someone as unorganised as you, perhaps. But my dear friend, that is what you did. You did it and you continue to do it out of Love. And my dear friend you will succeed IN ALL that you decide to do. You will show strangers, you will show your family, your friends and your children how to attain their hearts desires and live in peace, happiness and contentment. You will do this because this is the promise you made to your potential before you were born and you will hold yourself to your own promise.

LIST THREE (LONG-TERM)

1.
2.
3.
4.
5.

THE BEGINNING

That was when it all started for me. When I was twenty-two years old. That bizarre night was the very first time that I started to sincerely question why we continue to do the things we do even though they often don't work for us (cornflakes and marmalade in the eye will do that to you every-single time!)

I questioned all religions and wondered if a priest or any religious man has more right to Heaven on Earth, or Heaven in the afterlife, than a good-hearted man who has never heard of Christianity or Islam, but, nevertheless, was a kind, generous loving humanitarian who did his utmost to do no wrong, but occasionally failed, as most of us do.

It's my choice to believe in God. As *perhaps* selfishly that choice works well for me. It's a belief that helps with my stresses and my strains and my big and small decisions. I believe in a power that is mightier and wiser than I am. This amazing force has my welfare at heart helps me to suspend judgement and even a large degree of fear. This belief makes me feel like I'm sharing my workload and no task that is brought to me is too difficult. I feel I'm given guidance in my choices and inspiration in my actions. And even *'failure'* is a clever two-layered gift in disguise. The first layer is the *unattractive* layer that I receive now, which is always followed quickly or slowly by the *attractive* layer directly below the first. Of course I can't get to the second/good layer without passing through the first bad layer but that is the nature of *"failure."*

You may believe in a different God or none at all. The God that I believe in is not so vain that he wouldn't let you into Heaven because you never read the Bible. Ultimately, **it's not the books you read but the life you lead** and if I'm fortunate enough to end up… up there. I know that I will meet up with my with my Muslim, Jewish, Christian, Buddhist and Sikh friends and we'll all have a laugh and a cry about what's going on Earth. They're probably having a laugh and a cry up there right now.

People change religions everyday and none are struck down by lightning. People marry into different religions everyday and nature still allows them children.

All over the world people adopt new perspectives, different attitudes, alternate view points and their heads do not explode. Except that guy in the white suit last week at the supermarket, now that was pretty spectacular stuff (another little joke)!

Granted you are what you are, but please believe me when I say with my hand on my heart, that you are much, much, much more than that as well.

You, dear reader, have begun an amazing journey and now at last you can say this journey is truly yours. Your patience and your courage are to be rewarded at a time that is best for you but perhaps not of your choosing. May God and the entire Universe guide and bless your every step, every word and every thought. And may the waiting unlimited happiness and fulfilment that is yours, be uncovered by you soon.

Your friend,
Michael Doiley.

CPSIA information can be obtained at www.ICGtesting.com
Printed in the USA
LVOW04s0259240815

451274LV00023B/496/P

9 781607 460022